JUST A MINUTE
GLIMPSES OF OUR GREAT CANADIAN HERITAGE

JUST A MINUTE

GLIMPSES
OF OUR GREAT CANADIAN
HERITAGE

MARSHA BOULTON

McArthur & Company
Toronto

First published by Little, Brown and Company (Canada) Limited
This edition published in 1999 by McArthur & Company

Canadian Cataloguing in Publication Data

Boulton, Marsha
    Just a minute: glimpses of our great Canadian heritage

ISBN 1-55278-024-4

1. Canada — History — Miscellanea. I. Title.

FC176.B673 1999   971'.002   C99-930490-9
F1026.B68 1999

Cover Illustration: Rocco Baviera

Back Cover Design: Adams & Associates

Interior Design and Typesetting: Pixel Graphics Inc.

Printed and bound in Canada by Transcontinental Printing

McArthur & Company
322 King Street West, Suite # 402
Toronto, Ontario, Canada, M5V 1J2
10 9 8 7 6 5 4 3 2 1

TABLE OF CONTENTS

ACKNOWLEDGEMENTS

The Author acknowledges The CRB Foundation's Heritage Project for its generous support. Without their vision, no such idiosyncratic anecdotal retelling of historical events would have ever been produced.

Special thanks must go to Stephen Williams who conceived the notion of historical anecdotes for popular newspaper syndication and convinced the Project to support them.

For his unflagging intellectual and moral support, I would also like to thank the Project's Creative Director, Patrick Watson. His sense of humour about things historical is infectious.

For their commitment to the concept of a syndicated newspaper column about things historical I am indebted to Dr. Tom Axworthy, the CRBF's Executive Director, Ms. Ann Dadson, and Michael Levine who has, since the beginning, been a source of encouragement. Thanks also to Bruce Yaccato, producer of the "Just A Minute" television series.

Special credit must go to Dr. John Thompson of Duke University, who served as an unwavering and enthusiastic historical watchdog.

My personal thanks go to the many friends who have endured interruptions in polite conversation while I indulged a time warp and regaled them with some inexplicable minutae such as Robert Service's potato-eating habit.

Thanks also to people such as John Mellor, Barbara Laing, Wilma Coutts, and many, many others too numerous to mention, who shared their remembrances of historical events they saw first-hand. I owe a debt of gratitude to curators and archivists across the country who have provided source material and I commend the librarians of Wellington County and St. Catharines, Ontario for their patience and co-operation. Finally, I wish to thank my publisher, Kim McArthur. As she well knows, history can be an unrelenting task-mistress.

— Marsha Boulton

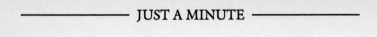

PART 1

ORIGINS

HUSH LITTLE SNORRI, DON'T YOU CRY

GENTLE BIRDS NO LONGER

WHOEVER HEARD OF A COUNTRY NAMED "BOB"?

SURVIVAL OF THE FITTEST

THAT AND A GLEEK WILL GET YOU A CUP OF COFFEE

THE SULTAN OF SWASH

CLOTHES DO NOT MAKE THE MAN

NEWFOUNDLAND NANA

AND THEN THERE WERE NONE

OH HOW WE DANCED ON THE NIGHT WE WERE CONSTITUTIONALIZED

GREEN SIDE UP!

HUSH LITTLE SNORRI, DON'T YOU CRY

Newfoundland, 1000 A.D. — How many people know that a Norse baby with the sleepy-sounding name of Snorri was born around 1000 A.D. in Newfoundland? Snorri is believed to be the first European child born in North America.

The name Viking actually hails from the Norse word for raiding, and the pillage and plunder of these fierce Scandinavian pirates was felt from the stone chapels of Ireland to the Byzantine cathedrals of Constantinople between 800 and 1000 A.D.

At a time when most European sailors scarcely dared to go beyond their own shores, the Norsemen had settled Iceland and the infamous outlaw Erik the Red had discovered Greenland.

It was Erik's son, Leif, who explored the seas even further west and brought his long, wave-skimming ships called *knorrs* to the "Land of the Flat Stones," which may be Baffin Island, and to the "Land of the Forests," possibly Labrador, and finally to the mysterious place called "Vinland."

According to the sagas, Leif and his men stayed for the winter in Vinland, where there was little frost and the salmon were larger and more plentiful than they had seen before. Commercial grapes as we know them would not have been in evidence, but the Norse words *vin* and *vinber* may be translated to include the multitude of wild berry species that still grow in the sheltered coastal bays. Other scholars suggest that *vin* referred to good pasture land, a valuable commodity to Norse settlers, who travelled with livestock in need of feed.

Leif's Greenlander brother, Thorvald and the respected Icelandic trader Thorfinn Karlsefni who was descended from the legendary Ragnor Shaggypants, made the first attempts to inhabit Vinland. They set out with four ships, 160 settlers, livestock and personal effects to colonize Vinland the Good.

They may have spent their first winter near Epave Bay, much further north than the more temperate climate described by Leif. In the spring, several parties set out to explore the coastline.

A saga tells the story of a chance encounter in which Thorvald was struck by the arrow of a *Skraeling*, the Norse name for the native inhabitants. His dying words now seem prophetic: "It seems we have found a good land, but are not likely to get much profit from it."

Confrontations between the Norse settlers and the Skraelings appear to evolved from great confusion, compounded by the Viking disposal to option warfare over communication.

On one occasion the Skraelings arrived at the settlement with intent to trade. A bull charged out of the bush and when the terrified natives sought shelter in the Norse huts, they were presumed to be attackers. Battles ensued between Vikings armed with swords and axes and Skraelings who fought with their sealing harpoons.

Discord and murder within the colonist groups led

the Vikings to return to Greenland, seldom to visit again. The sagas indicate that Snorri accompanied his parents. After his father died, his mother, Gudrid, undertook a southern pilgrimage, possibly to Rome. She returned to her homeland to find that Snorri had built a church for her and she lived as a nun for the rest of her life.

For centuries, no proof of Viking settlement in Newfoundland existed beyond the sagas that pre-dated Christopher Columbus' discoveries by 500 years. Finally, after years of study, a Norwegian group led by Dr. Helge Ingstad discovered the remains of a Viking settlement at L'Anse Aux Meadows, near Newfoundland's northern tip in 1961.

Today, there is a national park at the site where a Norse baby may have slept by a fireplace while his mother spun wool and sang Viking lullabies.

GENTLE BIRDS NO LONGER

Funk Island, Newfoundland, 1534 — When the playful puffins dig their Atlantic coast nesting burrows they still kick to the surface the occasional bone of their long extinct cousins, the great auk. Like the Mauritius Island dodo before it, the fate of the great auk of eastern Canada was sealed by the intrusion of man. Indeed, the final gasp of the auk came at the greedy hands of man in 1844. Three hundred years before, Funk Island off the New-foundland coast hosted a breeding colony of legendary proportion.

The great auk was the only flightless variety of its species, which includes guillemots, murres and puffins. It was a curious-looking sort of seabird that walked upright much like a penguin. While the seventy-five-centimetre-high bird may have trundled awkwardly on shore, in the water auks could "fly," propelling themselves rapidly with their rudimentary wings and steering with their powerful webbed feet to catch the fish and crustaceans that formed their diet.

They may have ranged from Greenland to Eastern Canada and as far south as Florida. Most of their life was spent in the water, and they are believed to have come ashore only during the breeding season, when the female would lay her annual, single egg after reaching maturity at four to seven years of age. The egg would be laid on bare rock. Both parents are presumed to have taken responsibility for its incubation, and the fledgling chick may have been ready to leave the nesting ledge within ten days of hatching.

Jacques Cartier noted the birds on his first voyage to the New World in 1534 when his crew stocked up on them at Funk Island. With an estimated 100,000 pairs, the island was home to the world's largest great auk colony.

"Some of these birds are as large as geese, being black and white with a beak like a crow," Cartier says in his diary. "These birds are marvellously fat. We call them Apponatz [spear-bills], and in less than half an hour our longboats were log-loaded with them. Each of our ships salted four or five casks, not to mention those we ate fresh."

The great auk proved to be a steady and easily harvested staple for early explorers. Their feathers were sold. They were boiled to make oil, used as bait for fishing lines and their eggs were a delicacy.

By the 1700s the number of great auks was seriously depleted as thousands of the helpless creatures were slaughtered by passing traders, who either clubbed them to death or simply marched them up planks onto their ships. Fishermen in Newfoundland and Labrador, as well as whalers from across the North Atlantic, joined in the slaughter.

In 1795, one observer wrote: "It has been customary for several crews of men to live all summer on the island for the purpose of killing birds for the sake of their feathers. If a stop is not put to that practise, the whole breed will be diminished to almost nothing." By 1800, that prophecy had come true and only a few scattered birds remained throughout their North Atlantic range. Such rarity placed them in great demand in Europe, where museums began clamouring for specimens.

One early morning in June 1844, possibly driven by a museum reward of about thirty dollars, a party of hunters went ashore on Eldey Island off the southwestern peninsula of Iceland and killed the last two great auks on earth. Reports indicate that the auks ran but uttered no cry and offered no fight, for they were gentle birds. Today, pickled organs from those very birds are preserved at the University of Copenhagen. All told, only seventy-eight stuffed specimens of the great auk remain. Funk Island, which still thrives as a breeding colony for seabirds, still bears the remnants of ancient stone pounds where the great auks were once impounded before slaughter.

Although it was man who physically killed the last of the auks, modern scientists speculate that extinction may have been their ultimate destiny due to changes in environmental and climatic conditions that could have effected their feeding and breeding grounds.

The sad thing is that we shall never know what could have been.

WHOEVER HEARD OF A COUNTRY NAMED "BOB"?

The New World, 1535 — We have a flag, an anthem, and a government, but whence this moniker "Canada?" The nation's appellation can be traced back to the Iroquois word *kanata* (meaning village). The symbolism is healthy enough, and the word has a nice ring to it, but the fact is that the naming of Canada resulted more from misunderstanding than intention.

The European who is credited with providing a name for our nation over 400 years ago is master French mariner and explorer Jacques Cartier. On April 20, 1534, Cartier left the French port of Saint Malo with two ships and sixty-one men. His Royal mission on behalf of King Francis I was: "to discover certain isles and countries where it is said there must be great quantities of gold and other riches."

Instead, after thirty-three days of sailing, Cartier sighted Labrador. His disappointment was palpable when he discovered little more than rock and trees. "I saw not one cartload of earth in all that northern coast," he wrote. "I believe that this was the land God gave to Cain."

Cartier's ships hauled south where they explored and charted what is now known as the Gulf of the St. Lawrence. That June, he landed on Prince Edward Island, which he found to be "the best-tempered region one can possibly see." Still in pursuit of gold, he sailed north off the coast of New Brunswick until reaching a large, warm-water inlet that opened into a bay that Cartier called *Chaleur* (French for "heat").

It was here that Cartier reported the first formal exchange of furs between Europeans and Indians, when two groups of Micmac people approached one of his long-boats in forty canoes laden with furs that they were anxious to trade. The sight of so many natives frightened the French, who motioned them away and responded to the Micmac's persistence with cannon fire. Although the Micmac were wary, they finally convinced the French that their mission was one of peaceful commerce. The nomadic Micmac had been trading with visiting Europeans for almost half a century. They were eager to barter furs for small iron tools and wares.

Upon his arrival in the Bay of Gaspé, Cartier was greeted by people from the Iroquoian village of Stadacona, who had come from the interior on a fishing expedition. Their chief, Donnacona, provided gifts and feasting.

On July 24, 1534, Cartier erected a thirty-foot, wooden cross on the shore. At the top, the words "Vive Le Roy de France" were carved in ancient lettering. The sight was unsettling to the Iroquois. Cartier explained, in sign language, that the cross was merely a marker.

Honest and direct communication was difficult, so Cartier took two of Donnacona's sons back to France to be trained as interpreters. Although he had not found the promised gold or riches, the King agreed to a second expedition.

The following spring, three ships left Saint Malo and Donnacona's sons ably guided Cartier past Anticosti Island

and up a broad river. On August 10, 1535, Cartier named the mighty river the St. Lawrence in honour of the saint whose feast day it was.

Proceeding up the river, Cartier finally reached a great fist of rock where he found the settlement of Stadacona, which became the site of Quebec City.

At this point, there is historic conjecture that Cartier was advised by his interpreters that the settlement at Stadacona was *kanata*, the Iroquois word for "village" or "community." Cartier, it would seem, thought it was the name of the whole country. The phrase "Kingdom of Canada" appeared in Cartier's journal on August 8, 1535. Subsequently, the name "Canada" appeared on the 1547 "Harleian" world map, which displayed the discoveries made during Cartier's second voyage.

Of course, there are other explanations for "Canada." Some have contended that Spanish explorers had sought gold around the Bay des Chaleurs. Finding none, they left after explaining to the natives: *aca nada*, which means "nothing here."

Alternately, the *Kingston Gazette* of 1811 suggested an even more fanciful proposition. The newspaper reported that the name Canada may have been derived from settlers in New France who were allowed only one can of spruce beer each day and "every moment articulated 'can a day'."

SURVIVAL OF THE FITTEST

Island of Demons, New World, 1542 — There was a penalty for falling in love in the New World. Law books were not among Jean-Francois de La Rocque de Roberval's belongings when he sailed to the newly-discovered territory which had been claimed in the name of France by Jacques Cartier in 1534. However, as the commander of an expedition to establish a colony, Roberval determined that the punishment for amorous indiscretion was banishment.

After an eight-week voyage, three ships with a cargo of 200 settlers, provisions, livestock and weapons sailed into the harbour of what is now St. John's, Newfoundland on June 8, 1542.

Roberval had invited his niece, Marguerite, to join him on the daring adventure. Unknown to him, a young stowaway had also joined the expedition and his sights were clearly set more on Marguerite than the New World.

While the ships were stocked with water and supplies, Marguerite and her young man spent three weeks roaming antediluvian Newfoundland hills, gathering berries, fishing for salmon, and making love. Throughout the romantic idyll, Marguerite's servant, Damienne, acted as a guard for the lovers.

Word of the affair infuriated Roberval, who considered Marguerite's indiscretion to be a deliberate disgrace of the family name.

En route to the St. Lawrence where Cartier had established a fort, Roberval marooned Marguerite, her lover and the servant on an uninhabited island known as Ile des Demons (the Island of Demons). It may well have been Fogo Island off the northeast coast of Newfoundland. In one account, Roberval is said to have banished the nameless young man and Marguerite begged to share his fate. In another, the young man chose to be with his disgraced beloved. Damienne, it seems, had no choice.

That summer, the outcasts built a cabin. Game, fruit and bird eggs were plentiful, but they were haunted by the night calls of the unfamiliar species of birds which had given the place its demonic name.

For eight months, they did not see a ship and Marguerite's young man became depressed and physically ill. He died shortly before their child was born. Undaunted, Marguerite applied her hunting skills, using a matchlock gun her uncle had provided to harvest wild food. She told her biographer that she became so skilled that on one day she killed three bears, including one that was "white as an egg," no doubt a polar bear that had drifted south on an ice pan.

After seventeen months on the island, the servant died and Marguerite's child soon followed. A year later, lonely but in good health, she was rescued by Breton fishermen who were astonished to find the bedraggled French noblewoman.

Ironically, Jean-Francois de Roberval's colony at Cap-Rouge, upstream from Quebec City, was a dismal failure. Many colonists suffered from hunger, filth, cold and scurvy before the expedition disbanded.

After her return to France, Marguerite de Roberval's triumphant survival in the New World was documented by André Thêvet, the Geographer Royal to King François I and it became popular reading.

One of those readers was Thevet's successor, Samuel de Champlain, who later helped establish a successful colony at Port Royal that was based on the theory that it was possible for settlers to live off the land. What started with a tragic love story set a pattern for survival in the New World.

THAT AND A GLEEK WILL GET YOU A CUP OF COFFEE

New France, 1684 — As the Intendant of the colony one of Jacques de Meulles' responsibilities was to supervise the operating budget and pay the troops. Apparently, he was a man who took his responsibilities seriously. So when the coin coffers were bare, he was determined to find a short-term solution, and he found it in a deck of playing cards.

Although Europeans were using paper money backed by gold bullion in the seventeenth century, colonists in New France relied largely on the barter system due to a scarcity of coins. Most of the settlers were subsistence farmers and they traded their goods and services for whatever they required. Such trading was formalized in September 1670, when a decree issued by the Sovereign Council set a standard for measuring the value of beaver pelts, moose hides and other furs. Although it may seem ecologically unfriendly today, one blanket could be purchased for eight wildcat pelts.

Members of the garrison were paid in coins which were sent from France, and in 1670 silver and copper coins were minted for specific use in New France. In the spring of 1684, the French government neglected to ship coins. This left de Meulles in an uncomfortable position, since the men under his command were kept busy with their military responsibilities and had not acquired the pelts to pay for their board and lodging.

In desperation, de Meulles determined to issue paper money based on playing cards endorsed by him, which would be redeemable the following year when coins would surely arrive. It was a bold gamble, but one that paid off.

Card playing was a popular activity in the barracks of Quebec City, where active games of "maw" involved elaborately illustrated cards with names such as Tiddy, Gleek, Tup-tup and Towser. De Meulles collected decks of durable cards and cut each one into four pieces, which he marked and stamped as "good" for specific amounts of currency under his seal and signature.

This imaginative solution to a shortage of coin worked quite well for many years and suffered vagaries typical of modern paper money, including a devaluation to half its face value in 1719. Thirty years later, the King of France authorised the issue of card money to be increased from 720,000 to one million livres.

The conclusion of the Seven Year's War in 1763 saw an end to playing card currency in favour of British sterling. A hodgepodge of currency followed including Nova Scotia provincial money, American dollars, Spanish dollars and U.S. gold coins.

Paper money was introduced in 1792 by the Canada Banking Company, but it lacked a certain credibility. It was considered to be about as valuable as a U.S. continental dollar, which was virtually worthless at the time. Coins were again at a premium during the War of 1812, and the government of Lower Canada issued paper "army bills" to purchase supplies.

In 1837, William Lyon Mackenzie signed the first

ten dollar note issued by the provisional government of Upper Canada. Swindlers issuing bogus, but colourful, three dollar notes were quick to follow.

Bank notes which were not backed by gold did not become legal tender throughout Canada until August 3, 1914, the day before Britain declared war on Germany. The rest is a crumpled history of bills folded in wallets at values dictated by global circumstance. In this nation, it all started with a deck of cards.

THE SULTAN OF SWASH

New France, 1690 — Even as he strode down the gang-plank, Governor Frontenac was a swashbuckling vision. His wig was perfectly curled and his scarlet hat sported an appropriate plume. He exuded courage and confidence and was determined to rule his colonial posting as a "high and mighty lord."

In fact, Louis de Buade, Comte de Palluau et de Frontenac was a bit of a poseur and deadbeat. Although he was the godson and namesake of King Louis XIII, and had earned a rank equivalent to that of a modern brigadier general, he also managed to amass a debt that has been estimated in excess of 800,000 livres (two million dollars). His arrival in Quebec in 1672 as the new governor was a highly-calculated career move that effectively blocked his creditors' attempts to seize his French properties.

Governor Frontenac was a man of many weaknesses. He was proud, vain, stubborn and impatient. All of these attributes, plus his agility in avoiding formal channels of approval for such items as the building of new fur trading posts, led to his recall to France after a decade.

In the years following his retirement, the colony of New France was eroded by weak leadership and Frontenac had once again accumulated vast debt. In 1689, sixty-nine-year-old Frontenac was returned as Governor of Canada to the delight of the colonists.

During his absence the Iroquois had allied themselves with the British and the *Canadien* colonists had come under constant attack. Shortly before his arrival, raiding Iroquois had killed twenty-four settlers and taken ninety captives at Lachine, Quebec.

Frontenac determined that the only way to defeat the British was to defeat them in the eyes of their native allies. He mounted a series of surprise attacks on outposts of the New England colonies that spread terror throughout the English frontier settlements. The tactics of this warfare were brutal. Both the British and the French offered rewards for scalps. In Massachusetts, the cry went out for revenge and an English fleet of thirty-four warships under the command of Sir William Phips set out from Boston to capture the French colony.

Frontenac made immediate plans to defend the fortress of Quebec, which was the gateway of the St. Lawrence and guarded the rest of the colony.

The siege of Quebec began on October 16, 1690. Hoping to avert a bloody assault, Phips sent his emissary, Major Thomas Savage, to order the government to surrender. At this point, Frontenac achieved a brilliant stroke of tactical deception.

Savage was blindfolded and led through the town to Frontenac's headquarters. Along the route, citizens and soldiers raised a great commotion, giving the impression of a large and willing garrison readied and eager for battle. Governor Frontenac received the emissary in a splendid room, surrounded by officers who wore their most elegant attire. The letter of demand from Phips was translated for

Frontenac. It ended with a request for a "positive" answer to be made by the sounding of a trumpet within one hour. But Frontenac was not about to blow any horn of defeat at the British. "My only reply to your general will be from the mouth of my cannon," was his blustering response.

The report delivered to Admiral Phips had the effect of a cold shower. It is even said that the message was punctuated by a cannon shot which took down the British flag.

The British launched an attack with 1,400 troops, but Frontenac's psychological ploy proved so effective that the solid stand of his small but valiant force of less than 500 *Canadiens* saw the British beat a hasty retreat after three days of siege.

Despite his human frailties, Frontenac proved himself a gallant Governor and his exploits have become the stuff of legend. When he died in 1698, one who knew him well wrote: "He was the love and delight of New France."

CLOTHES DO NOT MAKE THE MAN

Quebec City, 1738 — Long before the age of the sex change, an adventurous immigrant arrived in Quebec City as a male only to be deported as a female.

Esther Brandeau entered Canada as "Jacques La Farge." Ms. Brandeau was the first Jew to set foot in New France and she was eventually deported because she refused to convert to Catholicism.

The daughter of Jewish refugees from the Portuguese Inquisition who settled in Bayonne, France at the age of fifteen, Esther was shipwrecked while on her way to visit relatives in Holland. Following her rescue she decided not to return home, preferring adventure and the high seas.

She quickly discovered that her sex placed her at a disadvantage, so she disguised herself as a boy and signed on as a ship's cook in Bordeaux. Her ruse proved effective. Using the name Pierre Mausiette, she spent the next four years working variously as a tailor, a baker, a messenger boy in a convent and a footman to a military officer.

At nineteen, Brandeau adopted the name Jacques La

Farge and set sail for New France. Officials in Quebec City were immediately suspicious of the young Frenchman who bore a polished manner but wore ill-fitting clothes. No one could put their finger on anything specific, but the La Farge fellow was definitely "different."

Under questioning by the Maritime Commissioner, La Farge finally admitted that his name was assumed — as well as his gender. To further complicate the issue, Esther Brandeau added the revelation that she was also Jewish. For this admission, she found herself placed under arrest and confined at a hospital.

According to the policy of the French, non-Catholic settlement was prohibited in the tradition of one language, one religion, one loyalty and one monarch. Any non-Catholic immigrants were to be deported or converted.

Church authorities pleaded with Brandeau to convert. For months, they used every power of persuasion, cajoling and threat, but Brandeau was unyielding. A Jew she was, and a Jew she wished to remain.

After a year of fruitless effort, exasperated authorities gave up on the notion of ever converting Esther Brandeau. "She has been as much receptive as hostile to the instructions that zealous ecclesiastics have attempted to give her," reported the perplexed Intendant Gilles Hocquart. He was confounded by Brandeau's refusal to relinquish her religion and characterized her behaviour as "fickle."

In France, King Louis XVI was kept apprised of the bizarre situation in the colony. Finally, in 1739, on his express orders, Brandeau was shipped home at the expense of the French government. Historian Irving Abella, who documented Brandeau's New World adventures in his book, *A Coat of Many Colours: Two Centuries of Jewish Life in Canada*, reports that upon her return to France, Brandeau seems to have disappeared into obscurity.

Following the capitulation of the French in 1760, the British made the settlement of Jews in Quebec legal.

Seventeen years later the first permanent synagogue opened in Montreal. Sherith Israel was built on land donated by the family of Lazarus David, whose son, David, was the first Quebec-born Jew.

In 1871, the first Canadian census in the new Dominion of Canada included statistics on religion. Out of five religions listed, there were 1,333 Canadians of the Jewish faith. This figure more than doubled within the next decade as Canada accepted thousands of refugees from the anti-Jewish pogroms in Russia.

NEWFOUNDLAND NANA

Isle of Elba, 1815 — Under cover of darkness Napoleon Bonaparte was escaping from exile on the Isle of Elba when he slipped from a rock, fell into the sea and floundered. As the story goes, the sailors who were escorting him to a waiting ship could not find the military strategist. Fortunately, one of them had brought along his faithful Newfoundland dog. It is this distinctively Canadian canine who is credited with plunging into the water and towing the diminutive Emperor to safety from whence he returned to power and, ultimately, met his Waterloo.

Throughout history the Newfoundland dog has been perceived as a gentle giant and a life-preserver on four legs. It is one of only four recognized dog breeds originating in Canada, including the Canadian Eskimo Dog, the Nova Scotia Duck Tolling Retriever and the Tahltan Bear Dog. Although the Labrador Retriever bears a Canadian name, its breeding was refined in Great Britain.

Theories abound about the Newfoundland dog's origins. Some say that Norse explorers brought thick-coated, black "bear dogs" with them during the Vinland quest and these mated with indigenous dogs. Basque fishermen may have introduced ancestors linked to the Pyrennes mountain dog. Arguments have been made for bloodline links to everything from the English Water Spaniel to the now-extinct American Black Wolf. By 1610, when King James I granted John Guy the first charter to colonize Newfoundland, the Canadian Kennel Club warrants that the physical and mental attributes of the breed had been established.

Whatever quirk of fate created this water-resistant seventy-kilogram dog, the Newfoundland soon became an international status symbol, immortalized by some of the world's giants of literature.

Sir Walter Scott's favourite Newfoundland dog was named Mungo, and Robert Burns described an aristocratic Newf named Caesar in his 1768 poem *The Two Dogs*. Lord Byron's beloved Boatswain was held in such esteem that when he died in 1808, the poet constructed a brick and marble marker over his Sherwood Forest resting place.

In fiction, Nana, the faithful nursemaid of the Darling family in James Barrie's immortal, turn-of-the-century play *Peter Pan*, was played by the author's own Newfoundland. Charles Dickens delighted in the antics of his father-and-son team, Don and Bumble, and Fyodor Dostoievski included a Newfoundland in his novel *The Idiot*.

Above all the Newfoundland has served its masters as a working dog. For many years, sled teams of Newfoundlands transported mail and passengers to outport communities.

Their fine eye and pre-disposition to swimming makes them excellent retrievers, both of fowl and fish. When there was deep-water fishing off the southwest coast of the island, dogs were often kept aboard fishing boats to retrieve fish that slipped off the hook at the water's surface.

Newfoundland's have even served their own kind. When the Alpine rescue dogs at the Hospice of St. Bernard were almost wiped out by a distemper epidemic in

1856, the best of the breed from Newfoundland was used to re-establish the St. Bernard.

The best of the breed was also sought in 1901 when the Duke and Duchess of Cornwall and York (later King George VI and Queen Mary) visited Newfoundland and consented to accept a dog and cart for their children. "Isn't he a beauty," Her Royal Highness said graciously as she petted the Royal gift's massive head. "Begobs, ma'am," the trainer replied. "You won't find the likes of him nowhere." Local pride in the dogs has ensured the constancy and quality of the breed.

Bravery remains the Newfoundland's main claim to fame. In the folklore of dogdom, the Newf is credited with saving more human lives than any other breed.

One of the most remarkable of these instances occurred in December 1919 when the coastal steamer *Ethie* was wrecked near Bonne Bay off the Newfoundland coast. Rescue boats were out of the question as the waves raged on the rocky shores. At its owner's command, a Newfoundland dog swam through the surging sea to fetch a small rope that had been cast from the ship. The retrieved rope grounded a lifeline that saw all of the passengers rescued, including a baby who made the perilous journey in a mailbag.

Every pet is special, and the uniquely Canadian Newfoundland dog epitomizes the best traits of all companion animals. Lord Byron said it best in his tribute to Boatswain:

One who possessed beauty without vanity
Strength without insolence
Courage without ferocity
And all the virtues of man, without his vices.

AND THEN THERE WERE NONE

St. John's, Newfoundland, 1829 — When Shawnadithit died of tuberculosis in a St. John's hospital there were no relatives at her side. They were all dead.

It was the final chapter in a holocaust of atrocities that saw an entire people slaughtered like big-game hunting trophies.

Academics may suggest that extinction for these descendants of the prehistoric Maritime Archaic period was inevitable through European disease and ecological declines in food populations, but all of that remains conjecture because they were given no opportunity to adapt to anything except murder.

They were called the "Red Indians" by the Europeans, a name that followed from their custom of painting their bodies and their belongings with red ochre. From that it was a short trip to the pejorative term "redskins." Name-calling is far from the worst thing that happened to the aboriginals of Newfoundland known as the Beothuk or simply "The People." Genocide is the term most commonly applied. Historian Harold Harwood has described them as "the people who were murdered for fun."

The Vikings may have been the first to encounter the Beothuk. Sagas reveal encounters with at least two distinct native peoples, one of which was likely Dorset Inuit, and the other a taller, oval-eyed people which fits the Beothuk. Fifteen hundred years later, Jacques Cartier and John Cabot made contact. No one knows how many Beothuk lived throughout Newfoundland at that time, but the first recorded slaughter took place in 1613.

John Guy, Governor of the first English colony in Newfoundland, established trading relations at Trinity Bay in 1612. Things apparently went well. Guy arranged to return the following season to exchange goods for caribou hides and furs. When a ship entered the Bay during the approximate rendezvous period, the assembled Beothuk began dancing on the shore and launched a greeting party in ocean-going bark canoes. But it was the wrong ship. The celebration was interpreted as a war party. Grapeshot shattered the canoes. Some of the Beothuk men were killed and the rest fled.

This is not the first time such a "mistake" occurred, and it is the sort of calamitous error that might have found a reasonable resolution. However, before trading relations could resume, the Beothuk found themselves under assault by the Micmac who had migrated from Cape Breton Island and acquired guns from their French allies. According to one account, the French offered the Micmac a bounty on the Beothuk to encourage carnage and the Beothuk countered by beheading any white man they could capture.

Prior to such intrusion and skulduggery, the Beothuk had a peaceable lifestyle. Their deadliest weapons were bows and arrows, spears and harpoons. They spent their summers by the sea, collecting seabird eggs and harvesting fish. In spring and autumn, they hunted caribou along the

Exploits River. They wintered inland, where their homes were conical pole structures covered with sewn birchbark, which accommodated twenty to thirty people.

The Beothuk shared their possessions. Clothes, fire stones and amulets were their only private property. This concept contradicted that of the European settlers and opened the door for direct conflict when the Beothuk took to "liberating" items. But fishermen who suffered the consequence of vanishing salmon nets and other supplies, did not appreciate the cultural misunderstanding and decided to impose the death penalty. Europeans had already excluded the Beothuk from some of their seal and salmon hunting grounds. If men with guns had not killed the Beothuk, tuberculosis was a constant threat, coupled with malnutrition and starvation. Still, the threatened natives did not include guns in their pilfering, reportedly because they were fearful.

Until 1769, it was legal to kill the Beothuk and gun-butts were notched to keep tally of the kills. Then well-meaning administrators tried to provide deterrents, but the situation remained absurd. No court ever meted punishment for the killing of a single "Red Indian."

The carnage was unconscionable; men, women and children were massacred while their settlements were looted and burned. Hundreds were killed, and hundreds quite literally were all that was left of the Beothuk.

In 1823, a mother and her two daughters were captured and attempts to return them to their people failed. All but the youngest daughter died. There are reports of Beothuk sightings up to 1830, but extinction was inevitable.

Ironically, the surviving Beothuk became a servant at the home of a man who participated in the murder of the last Beothuk chieftain. Called "Nancy," Shawnadithit was about twenty-three when she was captured. In 1828, she moved into the home of William Cormack, who had founded the Beothuk Institute just in time to record whatever history and mythology the traumatised woman could impart.

One of the drawings Shawnadithit left behind shows a dancing woman. Impossible as it seems, the woman who knew as clearly as anyone could have that she was the last of her people, found it in her heart to portray an expression of joy.

OH HOW WE DANCED ON THE NIGHT WE WERE CONSTITUTIONALIZED

Quebec City, 1864 — In photographs, the Fathers of Confederation are a solemn lot, but beneath that paternal stoicism a good many apparently had "happy feet." In fact, dancing was a critical component in the passing of the seventy-two resolutions that formed the basis of the British North America Act.

For eighteen days in October 1864, delegates from English and French Canada, New Brunswick, Nova Scotia, Prince Edward Island and Newfoundland met around a crimson-clothed table in the reading room of the Quebec Legislative Council. Through the dreary and rainy days, they debated and fought over issues such as representation by population and the composition of the Senate. The same issues had been discussed by many of the same delegates the previous month in Charlottetown, following long debates within their own constituencies and legislatures.

One unusual attribute of the Quebec Conference was the invitation extended to the female family members of the male delegates. The sponsors went to great lengths to organize glittering nighttime balls for their enjoyment.

So it was that five wives and nine daughters of nineteen hesitant Maritime delegates earned the nickname "Mothers of Confederation," since the tireless politicians took every opportunity to waltz away any doubts about the wisdom of a united Canada. The rewards of their ebullient evening charm were reaped at the meeting table during the following days.

"All right! Confederation through at six o'clock this evening — constitution adopted — a creditable document — a complete reform of the abuses and injustices we've complained of," cheered Liberal delegate and *Globe* publisher George Brown in a hasty note from Quebec to his wife, Anne.

Still, it had been six years since Alexander Galt had originally introduced the idea of British North American union, and it would be one more Conference and more than two years before Queen Victoria would grant Royal Ascent to the British North America Act.

In fact, forming Canada's original constitutional Confederation was no easy two-step, and it bore its moments of disenchantment, discord and trod upon toes.

The unity of United Upper and Lower Canada was threatened as early as 1861 when Conservative George-Etienne Cartier insisted that "the two provinces coexist with equal powers."

Nova Scotian Joseph Howe, a once-and-future politician, published his nay-saying views in the press as "Botheration Letters." Three months after approval of the Quebec Resolutions he was predicting that Quebec would "escape from the confederacy" within five years.

Howe also tried to discredit Prime Minister Sir John A. Macdonald by sending the British colonial secretary an article George Brown had written for the *Globe* entitled "Drunkenness in High Places," which described an inebriated Macdonald clinging to his desk in Parliament to keep from falling.

Indeed Macdonald himself came close to missing Confederation entirely when he accidentally set fire to his bed during the final meetings in London.

Then there was the question of what to call the new nation. Macdonald favoured "Kingdom" of Canada, however there was British opposition to the notion of a colony having a title that would imply equality. The issue was resolved by New Brunswick Premier Leonard Tilley. He suggested "Dominion" of Canada after noting the seventy-second Psalm: "He shall have dominion also from sea to sea."

At the second reading of the B.N.A. Act the fandangos of its creators were confirmed. "We are laying the cornerstone of a great state," Colonial Secretary Lord Carnarvon announced in the House of Lords, "perhaps one which at a future day may even overshadow this country."

Ultimately, the dance of a federally united Canada began on July 1, 1867 when the British North America Act came into force. The Constitutional waltz continues. When it was patriated from Britain in 1982, Canadians were disco dancing.

The beat goes on.

GREEN SIDE UP!

The Canadian Prairies, 1890 — How did the pioneers build houses without any wood? They cut the lawn and stacked it, green side up. Called "soddies," they were literal grass-root structures, and they all shared one thing in common — they leaked.

Lumber was a very costly commodity to obtain on the prairies during the 1890s, when the Canadian government mounted a lavish advertising campaign in Europe to attract settlers by offering 160 acre sections of land "free" to anyone hardy enough to cultivate the land for three years.

Sod houses were modest structures which usually consisted of one room that measured about twelve by eight feet. The settlers cut the sod in "bricks" which were three feet long, two feet wide and six inches thick.

The tools that were used to accomplish this task were homemade, and the measurements were never precise. The sod was cut from a slough bottom where the grass roots were thick and tough. The slabs were stacked to a height of about eight feet, and the walls gradually settled into place.

Doors and windows presented a great building challenge. The single door entry was almost always lopsided, and those settlers who were clever enough to devise windows were the envy of their neighbours.

Occasionally light prairie willow brush was used to form the roof of sod houses, and even this was covered with sod. Inside the dark soddie houses, cloth was used to partition areas for privacy and white cotton covered the walls.

Walls were lined with planks, which were whitewashed monthly. With lumber financially out of reach, the planks often came from the wagons the settlers used to bring their basic goods over the deeply rutted trails that formed the only "road system" through Canada's vast western prairies.

Floors were generally pounded earth, which was swept daily after the dust had been laid with damp tea leaves. House-proud women spread hooked rugs on the floors. Managing a soddie household was a full-time occupation. Washing clothes was particularly difficult because the hard wellwater curdled the soap. Ashes or sand were used to scour steel cutlery.

A cast-iron stove was one of the few essentials that was store-bought and trade-name brands such as the Homesteader, the Rancher, and the Grand Jewel were the pride of each household. When firewood was scarce, which was most of the time, the stove was fuelled with buffalo chips or straw twists. Every day the homemaker tended the most valuable of possessions by rubbing it with Dome or Rising Son black lead polish to render a rich shine.

At planting and harvest time the soddie women joined their men in the field, hauling sheaves in their voluminous denim dresses and marching behind the oxen-powered ploughs. For food, they relied largely on the land and the livestock they brought with them.

Salt-pork was a continuous, and monotonous staple. Regular supplies included oatmeal, corn syrup and dried beans. A 100 pound bag of flour sold for about three dollars and sugar was five cents a pound. The dilemma was always finding a way to transport such items.

Of necessity, the homesteaders looked to the land to provide variety. The men hunted rabbits and game birds, fished the streams and sought out berry bushes.

The women became expert at gathering prairie species such as wild sage and onions. Tansy and yarrow plants were gathered for yeast, goldenrod provided dye, worm-wood was used for poultices and long, purple, licorice-coloured spikes of anise were turned into cough medicine.

There is no question that the life of the soddie settlers of western Canada was one of constant toil, peppered with turmoil such as drought and grasshopper invasions. Without the determination and innovation of those thousands of settlers who lived in little grass houses and made each soddie a home, the vast prairie wheat lands would never have become the bread basket of the world.

PART 2

HEROES, HEROINES & THE ODD VILLAIN

WITHOUT A COW

Beaver Dams, Upper Canada, 1813 — Laura Secord, whose name has become synonymous with boxed chocolates, was a genuine heroine of the War of 1812. However, her place in history was not recognized for many years, and even then her act of courage was often tethered to an imaginary cow.

Laura Ingersoll was born in Massachusetts in 1775. Her father, Thomas, who had been a patriot in the American Revolution, decided to take advantage of land grants offered in Upper Canada and moved his family to Oxford Township in 1793.

Laura married James Secord in 1797. He was a son of Loyalists and worked as a merchant. By 1812, the Secords maintained a modest home near Queenston Heights where they lived with their five children.

When the United States declared war against Great Britain, American troops marched on Canada and James Secord joined the Lincoln County Militia. Shortly afterward, he was wounded at the Battle of Queenston Heights.

While he was recovering under Laura's care, American officers occupied their home and Laura was required to cook for them. It was during one particularly boisterous and well-lubricated dining session that Laura apparently overheard the enemy outlining an attack on the British position at Beaver Dams, which was under the command of Lieutenant James FitzGibbon.

Before dawn the following day, Secord left her home to warn the troops. The thirty-two kilometre trek took at least eighteen hours. Throughout the interminably hot day, Secord avoided travelled routes and check-points. She forded streams, crossed snake-infested swamps and ended her journey by climbing the steep Niagara Escarpment.

At nightfall, she was discovered, exhausted, by a group of Mohawks, who formed the principal British fighting force. According to Secord's account, the encounter took place by moonlight and she was terrified. "They all rose and yelled 'Woman' which made me tremble," she recalled. She was taken to FitzGibbon, who reinforced his position.

With the Mohawks as their allies, the British were victorious. Five hundred troops surrendered and the consequence was a serious reversal for the Yankees. "Not a shot was fired on our side by any but the Indians," FitzGibbon wrote. "They beat the American detachment into a state of terror."

Laura Secord's trek did not become common knowledge for over forty years. FitzGibbon appeared to take total credit, and despite petitions on her behalf, Laura saw no reward.

In 1841, James Secord died, leaving his sixty-five-year-old wife virtually penniless and without a pension. Her bravery was finally officially recognized when the Prince of Wales, later King Edward VII, visited Niagara Falls in 1860. Secord's was the only woman's name on a list of 500 veterans of the War of 1812 which was presented to the Prince. In 1861, the Prince sent Secord 100 English pounds ($250). It was the only financial reward she received for her deed.

Fame came slowly, and often inaccurately. An early historian embellished the tale by adding a cow, which Secord was said to have used as a decoy. Following her death at ninety-three in 1868, several monuments were erected in her honour. In 1913, Senator Frank O'Connor chose her name for his new brand of chocolates. For many years the candies were marketed in white boxes adorned with a grandmotherly portrait of Secord and signed with a stylized signature.

Although her heroism may have had scant reward in her lifetime, as the wry joke would have it, had it not been for Laura Secord we might be eating Fanny Farmer sweets on Valentine's Day.

THE FLIGHT FROM FAMINE

Grosse Isle, Quebec, 1847 — In the mid-1800s, thousands of Irish orphans were adopted by French Canadian families. The potato famine in Ireland during the 1840s triggered the migration of over 100,000 Irish citizens to Canada in 1847 alone. Literally thousands of those poor souls died of typhus or cholera before they had a chance to settle. As a result, countless children found themselves alone, strangers in a strange land.

Most of the 1847 emigrants had been tenants on large Irish estates. In an over-populated country where the potato was the staple of the national diet, crops failed for two years in a row. Whole counties with poetic names such as Limerick, Tipperary, Clare and Cork were devastated by famine and its companion diseases.

In April 1847, more than 28,000 families were crammed into wooden transport ships bound for Quebec City, the main port of the St. Lawrence. Many of the passengers were stricken with "famine fever" (typhus) before they boarded and once they were crammed into narrow bunks below the deck the disease spread quickly.

Food and water aboard the ships were often in scarce supply. According to one observer the straw beds were "teaming with abominations" and the bodies of the dead were often left with the living, who were too weak to carry them to the deck. Of the 240 emigrants on board one ship alone, nine died at sea and another forty on arrival at the quarantine station of Grosse Isle, forty-six kilometres downstream from Quebec City.

Dr. George Douglas, the medical officer in charge, realized that the facilities were not adequate to serve the massive Irish emigration. He begged the government to increase his staff and facilities, but was able to add only fifty beds, bringing accommodation to 200 beds.

The oppressive heat of the summer worsened an already disastrous situation, and still the overcrowded ships kept arriving — 12,000 more immigrants disembarked on June 1st, another 14,000 a week later. The number of sick at the Grosse Isle hospital totalled over 1,000. New sheds were hastily erected, but both sanitation and shelter remained woefully inadequate. The sick were sometimes left on wooden slats on the ground.

By October, when the harbour closed, four doctors had died along with eighteen medical assistants. Two Anglican ministers and four priests were also felled by disease.

The immigrant toll was awful. A plaque erected by Dr. Douglas at a mass burial site notes: "In this secluded spot lie the mortal remains of 5,425 persons who, flying from pestilence and famine in 1847, found in North America but a grave."

During that summer, it has been estimated that 35,000 Irish died during their passage to Canada or shortly after their arrival. Ultimately, the immediate victims of this tragedy were the orphaned children. According to some estimates, the children outnumbered adults fifty-four to one.

Father Charles Felix Cazeau, Vicar General of the Diocese of Quebec, who was affectionately known as "the priest of the Irish," worked tirelessly to have the destitute children taken in by parish priests and placed in foster homes. An impassioned appeal was made to the rural French-speaking population, who answered the call from neighbouring villages.

Out of sympathy for the victims and their homeland, orphanages were careful to preserve the Irish identity of the children, keeping a record of their natural parents, their parish and county of origin, and the vessel that brought them over. The records also include many of the names and addresses of the foster families, most of them French Canadian.

In Quebec City alone there are records of 619 such adoptions. For example, five-year-old Pat Noonan who entered Canada from the ship *Odessa* in 1847, son of Patrick and Mary (née Coleman) of County Westmeath, was adopted by Louis Leblanc of St. Gregoire. In fact, all six of the Noonan orphans went to families in St. Gregoire and the records show that young Pat's five sisters married French Canadians.

In 1909, 9,000 people, many of them descendants of the survivors, gathered at Grosse Isle to dedicate a monument and ponder the meaning of the past.

Several French-speaking people bore witness to the events sixty-two years before by simply stating: "I was taken as a nameless child from this land [Ireland] and given to a family who did not let me forget that I was Irish."

THE LITTLE RAILROAD THAT COULD

St. Catharines, Ontario, 1851 — There once was a train that had no engine, no tracks but it carried 40,000 passengers. The Underground Railroad, which operated between 1840 and 1860, was the fanciful code name for a network of people with abolitionist sympaties who helped slaves escape to freedom in Canada. They were the "engine." The "tracks" followed invisible winding routes that stretched from the deep South to the Canadian border. The principal conductor of the "railroad" was a former slave named Harriet Tubman, who became known as "Black Moses."

In 1851, Tubman began using St. Catharines, Ontario, a small town near Niagara Falls and the American border, as her base. She made more than fifteen trips to the South over the following seven years rescuing more than 300 slaves, including her own elderly parents. By 1856, it was estimated that thirteen percent of St. Catharines 6,000 citizens were of Afro-American descent and nearly all of the adults were former slaves.

Tubman's daring accomplishments were not appreci-
ated by American slave owners and the Southern states
placed a $40,000 bounty on her head.

In 1850 the U.S. Congress passed a Fugitive Slave
Law, which made any northerner caught harbouring or
helping a slave liable to a fine of $1,000 and possible
imprisonment. Sympathizers offered shelter in barns and
houses called "stations." The men and women, white and
black, Canadian and American, who operated this secret
network of escape were its "agents" or "conductors."
Slaves were concealed by day and conducted to the next
station by night.

Struggling through wilderness brush on foot, the
"passengers" avoided travelled roads and lit no cooking fires
which might attract professional slave catchers who were
notorious for their cruelty. Few had a compass to guide
them. They followed the "drinking gourd" in the sky, the
Big Dipper which pointed the way north to Canada, where
slavery had been officially abolished in 1833. Dr. Martin
Luther King described Canada as "the North Star."

One of the slaves to find a new home in Canada was
Josiah Henson, who gained fame as the model for the title
character in Harriet Beecher Stowe's best-selling 1851
novel, *Uncle Tom's Cabin*.

Unlike the fictional slave protagonist who was beaten
to death by his master, Henson escaped from the Kentucky
plantation where he had been subjected to inhuman treatment. In 1830, he gathered a small parcel of food and all
the money he had (twenty-five cents) and fled north with
his wife and four children.

With other fugitives, Henson established a settlement
called Dawn (now Dresden, Ontario.) He became a minister and served as Commanding Officer of a black company
in the Essex Volunteers during the 1837 rebellion. In
1849, abolitionists in Boston published a seventy-six page
autobiographical pamphlet titled *The Life of Josiah Henson,*

formerly a slave, Now an Inhabitant of Canada, which is believed to have inspired Harriet Beecher Stowe.

Canadian acceptance of black refugees was something of an affront to the United States. It served notice of the emerging nation's independence as the groundwork was being laid for Confederation.

Enthusiastic support was offered by civil rights champions and abolitionists such as *Globe* editor George Brown through the Anti-Slavery Society, however discrimination was wide-spread. A recent history of St. Catharines notes that the general attitude was that "as they had once been slaves, they were somehow still inferior." Local attitude aside, when twenty-three former slaves were interviewed by reporter/historian Benjamin Drew the overwhelming description of their new homeland was as a place of "refuge and rest."

Throughout the 1850s, Mary Ann Shadd, a black teacher who was active in the anti-slavery movement, edited the *Provincial Freeman* in which she crusaded for racial equality and desegregation. Her father, Abraham, became the first black to hold public office in British North America when he was elected to a town council in 1859.

As Shadd wrote in a pamphlet entitled *Notes of Canada West* as a guide to black settlers: "No settled country in America offers stronger inducements to coloured people. The general tone of society is healthy, and there is increasing anti-slavery sentiment."

The legacy of the Underground Railroad is one of tolerance, compassion, and bravery. Its spirit is epitomised in the spiritual song "Follow the Drinking Gourd":

> *So long old Master,*
> *Don't come after me,*
> *I'm heading north to Canada*
> *Where everyone is free.*

BEYOND THE CALL OF DUTY

Long Point, Ontario, 1854 — The treacherous sandbars of Lake Erie have claimed many mariners to a watery grave. In 1827, three ships were wrecked at the same place off Long Point on the north side of the smallest of the five Great Lakes. Twenty-seven years later on a stormy November night, the fate of another shipwrecked crew lay in the hands of a twenty-four-year-old woman.

Abigail Becker was tending her two young children at her Long Point peninsula log cabin home that storm-tossed night. Her husband, a trapper, had gone to the mainland in the household's only boat when the heavily-laden schooner *Conductor* ran aground in the blinding sleet and snow.

The ship had keeled over by morning. When Becker spotted the remains, she saw eight surviving sailors clinging to the rigging. They huddled together on a small platform near the top of the foremast in frozen clothes.

Becker's first impulse was to build a large fire to signal to the men that help was at hand. She called for the children to bring a kettle and blankets. They gathered driftwood for a blaze, but Becker could see that the situation was growing desperate as the gale ripped and pushed the exhausted men.

The ship was lodged in the shallows hundreds of metres from the shore, and a yawl boat the men might have used as a lifeboat had torn clear. Although she did not know how to swim, Becker gathered her skirt and waded out into the breakers beckoning the men to come ashore.

The sight of her rallied the crew, and Captain Robert Hackett peeled off his jacket and boots to test the waters. "If I make shore successfully the rest of you follow," he is said to have told his crew. Using a rope, he flung himself out past the yard-arm and swam toward Becker who pulled him to the beach and sat him by the fire with a mug of tea.

One by one, Abigail Becker collected each exhausted crewman and lugged them to shore. Her crippled son was also trying to help when he was swept under, and the young woman found herself saving two lives in one trip.

Later, Lee Hays, the *Conductor*'s sixteen-year-old-cabin boy, described his own experience after taking the plunge. "I could feel the strong current pushing me from shore, so I began to swim with all my might. As the waves swept over me, I went under again and again. Finally I felt myself slip beneath the waves forever. Just at that moment, a powerful hand grabbed my arm. I coughed and spluttered as the woman heaved me over her shoulder. Icy waves crashed against us, but she never let go."

By the end of the day, seven of the sailors were ensconced at Becker's home. The cook, a non-swimmer, chose to remain on board. He was rescued by raft when the storm subsided the next day.

The rescue earned Becker the title "the heroine of Long Point." She was celebrated in magazine articles and poems. Queen Victoria sent her a personal letter and a gift of fifty pounds, and the Prince of Wales presented another gift when he was duck hunting on Long Point in 1860.

The sudden notoriety surprised Becker. "I only did my duty, just as anyone else would have done," she is reported to have said. She took a $500 purse presented to her by seamen and the family bought a farm near Port Rowan. Later, she used a gold medal presented to her by the Benevolent Life Saving Association of New York to barter at the local grist mill.

When the limelight dimmed, life's duty for Becker continued to be one of day-to-day heroism. All told, she adopted two children, bore eight of her own and acquired another nine through marriage.

She may have saved seven lives, but she raised nineteen.

FLAMES OVER THE SAGUENAY

Saguenay Region, Quebec, 1870 — On the morning of May 19, 1870, as Quebec farmers cultivated their land, a dark cloud rose on the horizon. Spring had come early to the area, but there had been scant rainfall and the farmers hoped that the edge of darkness was a sign of rain. To the north, near Lac St. Jean, a sulphurous yellow rain had soaked the ground that day. But instead of welcome moisture, the cloud was the sign of a raging fire that a westerly wind had spread to the bone-dry forest.

Like many of the forest fires that occur annually in Canada today, the inferno that would sweep through the Saguenay was caused by human carelessness. A family named Savard near the village of St. Félicien started a small brush fire that blew out of control. In a matter of hours, flames had destroyed everything over a distance of 150 kilometres from the Mistassini river, near Lac St. Jean, all the way to Baie des HaHa.

There was no time for the people to contemplate ways of fighting the fire. Animals were set loose and entire families fled to the banks of rivers and lakes, where they attempted to swim to safety. Others scrambled into makeshift dugouts or hid themselves in shallow basements and root cellars, while the fire raged above them with a suffocating heat.

Many families had small children and heroic efforts were made to save them. One father, Job Bilodeau, improvised a raft out of logs and branches that the fire had felled into nearby Lac Rond. He soaked the raft in water to prevent embers from setting it afire. After drenching himself and his two-year-old son, the pair set adrift while the shoreline lit up with flames.

At least five people died in the blaze, and many more suffered serious burns. One out of every three families lost everything they owned. By nightfall, the blaze had burned itself out and 5,000 people found themselves homeless and virtually cut off from the world in smoldering solitude.

A government representative reported to an inquiry that he found the area "a total and complete ruin." In the burned-out roadways he encountered weeping, half-clad families whose greatest fear was dying of starvation.

A disaster relief committee was quickly formed and $125,000 was collected and distributed to the victims, along with food, seed, clothing and other supplies sent in from parishes all over the province. The governments of Quebec and Ontario also provided assistance, and soon families were able to move from the crude huts they had carved from seared tree trunks into new homes.

The "Great Fire" left many scars, but despite the terrible toll, the resilient settlers of the Saguenay persevered. Fields were seeded again, barns were rebuilt, bridges and mills were reconstructed.

Ultimately, out of tragedy there came new hope. The destruction of the forest accelerated the clearing of the land for agriculture and contributed to the development of the entire region.

An ecological disaster transformed hundreds of hectares of northern Quebec into a scorched desolation which became productive farm land through the sheer determination of the early settlers. Some clouds do have silver linings.

ELEMENTARY, MY DEAR

Toronto, 1880 — Detective John Wilson Murray was the Canadian version of Sherlock Holmes. For most of his thirty-one-year career during the late 1800s, he was the only provincial police detective in a jurisdiction that extended east from Montreal to Rat Portage in Manitoba. He never gave up on a case and his tenacity earned him the nickname "Old Never-Let-Go."

Murray was born in Scotland in 1840 and moved to New York as a child. At seventeen, he enlisted in the United States Navy and he had his first taste of detective work during the Civil War. In 1862, he uncovered a complicated plot to free 4,000 Confederate prisoners.

After working as a special agent for the Navy he joined the Erie police force and, ultimately, came to Canada as Head of Detectives for the Canadian Southern Railway. In 1874, Ontario Attorney General Sir Oliver Mowat persuaded him to accept the position of Provincial Detective of Ontario.

Murray proved to be a tireless investigator who was

far ahead of his time in scientific criminal detection. Many a conniving soul found themselves convicted literally by their soles, since he was one of the first detectives in the world to realize the importance of footprints. He regularly requested an autopsy on murder victims and had clothing and murder weapons chemically tested for clues.

Between 1875 and 1880, counterfeiters embarked on a bold effort that sent over one million dollars in phoney bills into circulation throughout North America. The plates used to make the bills were so finely crafted that even the bank officials could not identify the fakes. In the far north-west $200,000 of such money was used to pay for furs that were shipped to England, Montreal and New York.

After contacting known "con" men in New York, Murray determined the bills to be the work of John Hill and Edwin Johnson, who were masterful engravers. After discounting Hill as an active suspect, Murray spent months tracking Johnson and his family to Toronto.

He staked out the Johnson house, and began conducting covert interviews with everyone from the family's butcher to the milkman to determine patterns of behaviour.

Everything appeared normal, until one day Murray followed Johnson on a boozy, bar-hopping session from Toronto to rural Markham. After many stops, the tipsy Johnson paid for a drink with a counterfeit one dollar bill, and continued to do so at various stops, culminating in a four dollar purchase of a necktie. Johnson was arrested.

Plates valued at $40,000 were unearthed in a north Toronto woodlot, where they had been carefully wrapped in oilcloth and encased in a protective coating of beeswax. There were twenty-one separate copper plates used to recreate seven different bills, including a U.S. five dollar note. Johnson's wife and seven children had all been involved in the creation and distribution of the phoney money, which was printed only once a year and quickly turned over to wholesale dealers known as "shovers."

Johnson's fatal flaw was his penchant for using the counterfeit money when he was inebriated. His nemesis, Detective John Wilson Murray, noted: "Crime lost a genius when old man Johnson died."

THE SAINT OF DAWSON CITY

Dawson City, Yukon Territory, 1897 — Those who knew Father William Judge sometimes claimed he had a "luminescent"quality, but those who met him for the first time often thought he looked more like a cadaver. For his part, the Jesuit priest placed small value on appearances. "I remember his telling, with a chuckle, that one season while wandering in the wilds he had eaten so many rabbits that he felt his ears each morning when he awoke to see they weren't growing longer," recalled miner Karl Kaiser.

Judge was born in Baltimore in 1850 and worked as a clerk in a planing mill before deciding on a religious life. In 1890, he joined the Rocky Mountain Mission in Alaska.

He was ministering at a remote mining town called Forty Mile when George Carmack, Sookum Jim and Taglish Charlie registered the first claims on a salmon stream the native people called "Throndiuck," (meaning Hammer Water), and which later became "Klondike." Four months after their discovery, Father Judge sent a letter to his brother that carried one of the earliest messages of the find to the "outside." He noted that the discovery near Dawson City was "one of the richest and most extensive gold fields ever known." Predicting a general stampede of gold-seekers that spring, he promptly acquired a three-acre site for a church and a hospital.

"The stampeders from Forty Mile to the Klondike in the winter of '96-'97 remember overtaking a solitary and feeble old man with a single sled rope over his shoulder and a single dog helping the load along," recalled the *Klondike Nugget*. In this humble guise, Father Judge made several trips between Dawson and Forty Mile.

That summer, he replaced his tent hospital with a two-story log-structure, followed by a church building complete with an organ. In November, he reported that 168 miners had been treated for everything from frostbite to scurvy, but despite the wealth of gold, the main topic of conversation in Dawson was "grub," and everyone was trying to secure enough food to last the winter. "If men would do half as much for heaven as they would for gold, how many saints there would be, and how much more real happiness in the world," wrote Judge. By the following spring, Dawson had grown to become the largest city west of Winnipeg and the atmosphere was hardly godly.

In June 1898 the church burned to the ground after Judge left a candle burning when he was called to the hospital during evening prayers. Dawson citizens turned out en mass to form a bucket brigade to save the neighbouring hospital. "It is a judgment on me," Judge shrugged. "I built the church too small. I had too little faith."

Judge immediately set about constructing a new church. It was entirely financed by the "Klondike King" Alex McDonald, who later used the donation as leverage to achieve an audience with the Pope.

When a typhoid epidemic struck in the summer of 1898, Judge went into debt to construct a three-story addition to the hospital. Soon even the halls and aisles were filled with cots. Six sisters and thirty-four employees were kept busy day and night. In addition, an average of 500 attended Sunday Mass and miners continued to pour into Dawson. "I fear there will be much suffering here this winter," Judge wrote. "There are thousands still in tents, and winter is on us."

That December arrangements were made for a "minstrel" entertainment to raise funds for the hospital. It was a sober affair, since Christmas fell on a Sunday and even in wild and woolly Dawson saloons and dance-halls were closed on Sundays. When Judge thanked the audience for helping the hospital a five-minute ovation followed, leaving "the grand old man of Dawson" heartily embarrassed.

Judge had always appeared to be older than his years. He was only forty-eight when he succumbed to pneumonia on January 16, 1899. On the day of his funeral flags flew at half-mast and stores closed. The church was draped in mourning, and hours before the ceremony the church filled to capacity. A miner who knew him later wrote: "He died, undoubtedly the richest man in all gold-mad Dawson for there was not a soul within the valley of the Yukon not made richer for the heritage he left us."

LION OF THE YUKON

Dawson City, Yukon Territory, 1898 — Superintendent Sam Benfield Steele of the North-West Mounted Police was as square of jaw and as forthright of conviction as Dudley Do-Right. He was a lawman who could bring order out of chaos, which was just what Prime Minister Wilfrid Laurier's government had in mind when Steele was dispatched to preserve peace on the Canadian side of the border during the Klondike Gold Rush.

The situation was ripe for trouble. In Skagway, Alaska on the American side of the border, gangster Jefferson Randolph "Soapy" Smith and his gang of thugs had a stranglehold on all things outlaw. "It seemed as if the scum of the earth had hastened here," noted one traveller. Steele, himself, found it to be "little better than hell on earth," a place where "robbery and murder were daily occurrences." Such behaviour would not be countenanced in Sam Steele's jurisdiction.

Steele made his first indelible imprint on the *cheechakoos* (tenderfoots) in the spring of 1898. He had established headquarters at Lake Bennett, where a tent city of more than 10,000 "argonauts" was waiting for spring break-up to free the river for the final leg of their journey to Dawson. By the time he arrived, about 150 boats had been wrecked in perilous rapids and at least five people had drowned. "Many of your countrymen have said that the mounted police make up the laws as they go along," announced Steele. "I am going to do so now for your own good."

With that, Steele established Mountie checkpoints and everything that attempted to float toward Dawson was inspected for seaworthiness. Women and children walked around the rapids. No more lives were lost.

The thousands who made it to Dawson City had to first pass muster with Steele's border posts on the legendary "Trail of '98." Customs duties were collected, handguns were confiscated and anyone who did not have the requisite 522 kilograms of food was turned back. Unruly intruders into Canadian territory were dealt with firmly.

One night Steele heard two shots near his cabin. The culprit was brought before Steele, who found marked cards and loaded dice in his saddlebags. "I'll have you know that you can't lock up a United States citizen and get away with it," the gunman boldly announced.

"Well seeing you're an American citizen, I'll be very lenient," replied Steele. "I'll confiscate everything you have and give you half an hour to leave town."

Amid the carnival ambience that marked the tent city that billowed at Dawson, Steele was a force of reason. What he initially found to be "a city of chaos" was quickly whipped into an orderly state, complete with a board of health and a dutiful respect for Sunday. Prostitution was confined to a red-light district, gambling was licensed, and comedians were prosecuted for disparaging remarks about the Queen. There was still plenty of room for "whooping it up." Indeed, in his 1958 book *Klondike*, author Pierre Berton notes that during the '98 season 120,000 gallons of liquor were imported into Dawson. But at the peak of the Rush, Steele reported: "Only three homicides have taken place, none of them preventable."

Something so simple as a monetary punishment for behaviour outside of the law would have been too easy in a community where fortunes were made (and lost) overnight. When Steele imposed a fifty dollar fine on a gambler, the response was often laughter. Steele's response was to add sixty days labour on the wood pile. "Have you got that in your vest pocket?" he would ask.

Soon Dawson boasted a stack of firewood nearly three kilometres long. Rounders who really irritated Steele earned a "blue ticket," which banished them from the town and curtailed their lucrative prey on newly-rich miners.

When Sam Steele roared, people listened. In political matters, however, the "Lion of the Yukon's" direct approach may have been his Achilles heel. When he tried to clean up the corrupt practises of bureaucrats, the Tory Steele ran up against Liberal powerhouse, Sir Clifton Sifton, who had friends with vested interests in securing powerful liquor licensing commissions and meat contracts.

On September 8, 1899, Steele was relieved of his command in a terse telegram signed by Sifton as the minister in charge of Mounted Police affairs.

Protests and petitions from the citizens of Dawson were to no avail. When Steele left town, prospectors, piano-players, dancers in petticoats and out-and-out whores lined the wharf. The departing red-coat was judged by the *Klondike Nugget* to be "by all odds the most respected man in the Yukon."

PAYING THE RENT

St. Anthony, Newfoundland, 1908 — When it came to the service of Newfoundland and Labrador, Dr. Wilfred Grenfell was simply irrepressible. He confounded bureaucrats, angered merchants, enraged religious leaders — but he got the job done and the people loved him.

The job was never a singular issue for Grenfell. After graduating from medical school in London, he joined the National Mission for Deep Sea Fishermen serving aboard ships from the Bay of Biscay to Iceland. In 1892, he volunteered to investigate living conditions in coastal Newfoundland and Labrador. What he discovered was a large job to be done.

Poverty and disease were rampant. Merchants exploited the half-starved population and housing was seldom more than a dirt-floored hut. From the deck of his floating mission, Grenfell treated 900 patients during his three-month cruise. Most had never seen a "real" doctor, relying instead on folk cures that were no match for diseases ranging from tuberculosis to beri-beri.

Returning to England, the young doctor was determined to raise funds for proper medical facilities. Although the Mission found his zeal incorrigible, his administrative skills inadequate and his exact location unchartable, the Grenfell charm was inescapable.

He toured England addressing the desperate need he had seen. Two doctors, two nurses and enough money for two hospitals accompanied him on his return to Labrador. Then he set off to raise more money. He was particularly skilled at plucking the pockets of Americans from the Eastern seaboard, dispersing funds as he saw fit from his headquarters in St. Anthony, Newfoundland.

Grenfell's resolve was inspired by the evangelical ideology of "muscular Christianity," which favoured expressing religious beliefs through action. "The service we render to others is really the rent we pay for our room on this earth," he once noted.

Grenfell was constantly struggling to pay that rent. Money that poured in from his tours poured out almost immediately as he added facilities to hospitals, established cooperative stores, industrial workshops and experimental farms. To assist him, he accepted volunteer students during the summer. His WOP program (Workers Without Pay) saw the likes of the young Nelson Rockefeller and Henry Cabot Lodge performing all manner of menial tasks.

Because he was good at it, fund-raising became Grenfell's preoccupation. In fact, it has been suggested that Grenfell's bedside manner may have been the best aspect of his physician's skills, but his commitment to attend a young patient suffering from blood poisoning nearly cost him his life on Easter Sunday, 1908.

In a move which hindsight reflects as foolhardy, he was taking his dog team over a short-cut across Hare Bay headed for Brent Island when the ice beneath him began turning to slush less than half a kilometre from land. What followed was a series of dives and leaps from one ice pan to the next, as an off-shore wind blew Grenfell and company slowly out to sea.

To avoid freezing, he sacrificed three of his sled dogs. Using their skins as blankets and windbreaks, he huddled with the remaining dogs throughout the night. Rescue seemed remote, but he constructed a flag using a piece of his shirt tied to the frozen legs of his dead dogs.

By a sheer stroke of luck, Grenfell's pitiful presence was spotted by a seal hunter as night descended. Early the next day, rescuers in a small boat risked their own lives through the hazardous ice pans to reach Grenfell, whose "pan" had dwindled to packed snow.

Typically, Grenfell turned the tale into a instrument to raise funds. *Adrift on an Ice-Pan* became a best-seller.

Although several of his ventures were abysmal failures, including the importation of 300 Lapland reindeer, the community of St. Anthony's prospered in everything from his introduction of cottage industries to a much-needed orphanage. It became the home of a mission in his own name, but still there was controversy.

Grenfell raised the ire of the Protestant and Catholic clergy when he opened Newfoundland's first inter-denominational school in 1909. As a Justice of the Peace he rendered his wrath freely to bootleggers. Politicians feared for the image (and the credit rating) of the colony when Grenfell publicly decried the squalor of the native people and the permanent residents known as livyers.

Sir Wilfred Grenfell, knighted in 1927, stood his ground against all comers for forty-five years in the service of the people. He resigned as superintendent of the International Grenfell Mission in 1937 and spent his retirement in Vermont. When he made his final visit to St. Anthony in 1939, the whole town wept when he left.

NEIGHBOURS IN ARMS

Western Front, 1915 — Lest we forget the valour and horror. After World War One, the city of Winnipeg changed the name of Pine Street. Why? To honour the individual heroism of three soldiers who, coincidentally, all lived on that quiet residential street. Pine Street is now called Valour Road in their honour.

The "neighbours" — Frederick William Hall, Leo Clarke and Robert Shankland — faced the horror of World War One with such valour that each of them won the nation's highest award for courage, the Victoria Cross.

At the outbreak of the war on August 4, 1914, Canada's "army" consisted of a mere 3,110 men in uniform and 74,213 part-time militia. The navy boasted two ancient cruisers. Experienced officers and drill instructors were in short supply. Still, there was a national will to "get on with the job," and soon recruits numbered in the hundreds of thousands.

Early in 1915, the first Canadian troops moved across

the English Channel and into battle. Their first engagement was at Ypres, Belgium and Winnipeg's Sergeant-Major Hall was there. The Allies, including twelve Canadian battalions, were outnumbered two to one. On the morning of April 24, 1915, Hall and his company were pinned down in the trenches by heavy artillery fire.

The men could hear the groans of an injured soldier on the battlefield.

Rescues were usually attempted under cover of dark, but this time Hall and two volunteers determined to try it in broad daylight. The volunteers were immediately wounded. After helping them back, Hall determined to accomplish the mission alone. He crossed the battlefield through a hail of bullets. Then, while trying to bring his wounded comrade to safety, Hall caught a bullet in the head and died instantly.

Better than one in five Canadians who participated at Ypres were listed as killed, missing or wounded. It was a horrific initiation to battle, and one that was to set a pattern of endurance, courage and bloodshed.

Late in the summer of 1916, Canadian troops moved to the rolling hills of the Somme, where a battle had been in progress for several months. The Germans called it "the Bath of Blood." It was here that the Canadians confirmed their steadfastness under the worst conditions of warfare. Corporal Leo Clarke was there.

In the mud-filled trenches, Clarke found himself alone and under attack by twenty enemy soldiers. Instead of surrendering, he attacked, emptying his revolver twice and then firing a German rifle he picked up from the ground.

In the stuggle that followed, a German officer bayonetted him in the knee. Wounded and bleeding, he kept up the attack. When the enemy fled, Clarke pursued them, killing four and taking a prisoner. Though he was ordered to the hospital, Clarke returned to battle the next day. He died in action a month later.

There were other battles in that tortured landscape — Vimy Ridge, Mount Sorrel, Courcelette, Amiens and Beaumont Hamel. Then there was Passchendaele, where Lieutenant Robert Shankland earned his Victoria Cross.

From August through November of 1917, the Allies fought in a sea of Belgian mud. The terrain was below sea level and drainage systems had been destroyed by bombardment. Heavy rains had reduced the ground to an impenetrable bog. Guns sank to their axles and horses to their bellies. Soldiers died relentlessly.

Shankland led his men to a forward position which they held during a fierce counter-attack. Knowing that an accurate description of his company's position was critical to the Allied battle plan, he crossed the battlefield alone to deliver the information. He then rejoined his men and carried on until the end of the bloody battle in which 16,000 Canadians made the ultimate sacrifice. Of the three Victoria Cross recipients from Valour Road, only Shankland survived the war.

More than 60,000 young Canadians were dead before the war ended in victory on November 11, 1918. On that day, a stillness descended over the Western Front, and a soldier from New Glasgow, Nova Scotia recalled hearing a bird singing. He wondered how it had survived.

WHEN SHIPS COLLIDE

Halifax, Nova Scotia, December 6, 1917 — The largest manmade explosion prior to the detonation of the atomic bomb occurred in Halifax Harbour during the First World War. It was not an act of war, it was an accident. The Halifax Explosion is the largest disaster in Canadian history. When two ships collided, the explosion was *felt* for over 320 kilometers.

There was a thin coat of snow on the harbour slopes that crisp winter day in late 1917. While the citizens of the booming wartime port travelled to work and school children readied for a day of studies, the French freighter *Mont Blanc* made its way toward the inner harbour. At the same time, a Norwegian steamer, *Imo*, was coming out of the narrows.

As a result of crossed passing signals, which may have been caused by the language barrier between the English and French crews, a midstream collision occurred at 8:00 A.M.

Although the ships drew apart without much damage, the *Mont Blanc* was carrying a devil's brew. In its hold there was 2,335 tons of picric acid, 203 tons of TNT and 10 tons of gun cotton. Highly inflammable benzene, stored in tins on the deck, began to burn with a flaring blue flame. The captain and crew of the *Mont Blanc* promptly took to their lifeboats, while their burning ship drifted toward one of the Halifax piers.

On the dock, most people were not aware that the burning ship was a floating bomb. Factory workers, stevedores, mothers and children rushed to the best vantage points to watch. The town fire department dispatched its new chemical engine and two boat parties fought the fire.

Train dispatcher Vincent Coleman was discussing the fire when a sailor burst into his office and announced that the ship was bound to explode. Coleman tried to warn the onlookers, when suddenly he remembered that a passenger train carrying 700 people was scheduled to arrive shortly. He returned to his post to telegraph a life-saving message.

At 9:05 A.M., the explosion came. A pillar of white smoke rose eight kilometres into the sky, unfolding into a gigantic toadstool. The *Mont Blanc* was blown apart and the *Imo* ran aground. A tidal wave swept the shore.

The force of the blast was strong enough to hurl a clock out of a tower at Truro, 100 kilometres away. In Halifax and Dartmouth, wooden buildings and homes collapsed, killing or burying the inhabitants who had barely finished stoking their morning fires. Doors blew off their hinges, and glass blasted from windows in jagged arrows. Schools and churches were demolished. Fires raged.

At the railway station, the glass-and-iron frame roof dropped in on the platform and tracks. Dockyards were shattered, foundries were ruined and a smashed brewery poured a river of beer into the harbour.

A blizzard howled that night, while 6,000 people left homeless by the blast crouched and huddled in any available shelter to survive the storm that followed.

The scene was as brutal and devastating as any

wartime carnage. The Halifax Relief Commission estimated that 1,963 people were killed, 9,000 were injured and 199 people were blinded. Makeshift morgues were set up to try to identify the dead and mass funerals were conducted, while the stunned citizenry rallied to rebuild.

Tragedies can bring out the best and worst in people. Some tried to take advantage of the explosion by looting, while others, such as dispatcher Vincent Coleman, sacrificed their own lives to save others. Doctors and nurses rushed to the scene and substantial help was soon on its way from outlying towns and neighbouring provinces. Halifax's historic rival, the state of Massachusetts, sent a complete relief expedition. Overall contributions totalling thirty million dollars poured in for relief and construction efforts.

Homeless Haligonians lived in temporary tents and patched together housing. Lumber was at a premium and glass was scarce during wartime, so construction was makeshift and citizens covered their windows with tar paper throughout that bleak winter.

Today the North Halifax Memorial Library stands as a monument to the victims of the tragedy. The half-ton shank of the *Mont Blanc*'s anchor still lies where it landed, three kilometres from the explosion, and at least 125 unidentified victims are buried in a common grave at Fairview Cemetary.

HUMAN ENGINEERING IN AN UNSEEN WORLD

Toronto, 1918 — There was no moon in the autumn sky over Hemmel Hill in Belgium as Lieutenant Edwin Albert Baker of the Sixth Field Company of Engineers reconnoitred the cratered landscape, laying a communication line between Canadian units on the frontlines and their farmhouse headquarters. The year was 1915. Baker was twenty-two, a farm boy from Kingston, Ontario who had earned his electrical engineering degree at Queen's University.

He was inspecting a caved-in trench when the sharp crack of rifle shots and machine-gun fire filled the air. One bullet from a German sniper creased the bridge of Eddie Baker's nose, destroying both of his eyes. He was the first Canadian officer to lose his sight in World War I.

"Now don't worry about me," Baker wrote to his parents, while he recovered and underwent therapy in London. At St. Dunstan's rehabilitation hostel, he adopted the philosophy of the institution's founder, Arthur Pearson: "Nothing should be done for a blind man, if he can possibly do it for himself."

Baker studied Braille, typing and business administration before returning to Canada. "Please, mother, don't ever do that again," he said gently, when he found that his "welcome home" roast beef dinner had been cut into pieces for him.

Through "Black Jack" Robinson, editor of the *Toronto Telegram*, he received an introduction to Ontario Hydro chairman Sir Adam Beck. Both men were impressed with the ernest young man. Baker ultimately married Robinson's daughter. At Ontario Hydro, he worked his way from the typing pool to a trouble-shooting, data collection position.

Baker became involved in working for the blind community when he discovered that Canada's only Braille library in Toronto was slated to close due to lack of funds. With the help of five friends and the assistance of the Toronto Women's Musical Club, the library was saved and moved to new headquarters.

Informal meetings at the library led to discussions about the need for a national organization for the blind in Canada. Such a group would extend itself into the community to help with the care, training and employment of the blind, as well as working to prevent blindness.

The Canadian National Institute for the Blind received its charter in 1918. Eddie Baker was its first vice-president, and five of the seven founding members were blind.

At first, the CNIB consisted of two small shops where men and women made brooms and sewed. Then, with government backing, Baker established the CNIB's Pearson Hall Training Centre where war-blind veterans were taught how to walk and function in an unseen world.

Baker went on to design training programs to help other blind Canadians. As head of the CNIB, he arranged for a range of services from vocational schools to seeing-eye dogs, as well as residences for the aged and public treatment clinics. Braille services were established, "eye banks" created and research launched into the causes and treatment of blindness. In areas of education reform and pensions, Baker was a leader.

Baker received many honours in the course of his career, including the Croix de Guerre, four honourary law degrees, the Order of the British Empire and elevation to the rank of colonel. For thirteen years he served as president of the World Council for the Welfare of the Blind, co-ordinating the activities of forty-seven nations.

"By a trick of fate, I found myself transferred from my proposed career as an electrical engineer to one which might be termed human engineering," Baker once noted.

GONE INDIAN

Temagemi, Ontario, 1930 — He wasn't a grifter in the classic sense; he grew into his con and stayed with it for the duration. Among other things, he was a drunk, a fraud, a philanderer, a bigamist, and a wife-abuser — but he liked beavers, a fact that stood him in good stead with English Royalty and posterity.

The author known as Grey Owl had other good qualities, such as his inordinate love and understanding of the wilderness and its inhabitants. When he wrote about nature, he wrote about what he knew and infused his stories with an essential sincerity that defies the make-believe mask of the Noble Savage that he wore to his death. His was a lifetime of performance art.

Grey Owl told anyone who would listen that he was a half-breed, born in Mexico to a Scottish-American father and an Apache mother. In fact, he was plain old Archibald Stansfield Belaney from Hastings, England, the son of a dipsomaniac and his teenage bride. He was raised by aunts, but even as a child he apparently acted out his fantasies. A history of the English grammer school he attended describes eleven-year-old Archie as "a delicate boy but full of devilment; and fascinated by woods and wild animals... What with his camping out, his tracking of all and sundry, and wild hooting, he was more like a Red Indian than a respectable Grammer School boy."

Disillusioned, confused and spellbound by the romantic tales of James Fenmore Cooper, Belaney came to Canada in search of adventure when he was eighteen years old. By 1930, the war veteran, trapper and forest ranger had completely assumed the mantle of the Noble Savage and become Grey Owl, or Wa-Sha-Quon-Asin meaning He Who Flies By Night. In fact, by this time Belaney had demonstrated his "fly by night" prediliction to several wives.

Belaney began writing under his birth-name, and selections from his diary as a trapper and forest ranger first appeared in *The Hastonian* in 1913. Sixteen years later, his first "professional" magazine article appeared in the British weekly, *Country Life*. He was encouraged to write more, and gradually began an elaborate process of configuring himself as a bona fide Indian. In a native ceremony, he married an Iroquois woman eighteen years his junior. Anahareo, who joined Grey Owl in the wilderness of Temagami instead of fulfilling a scholarship to Loretto Abbey (a toney private girls' school in Toronto), urged him to quit trapping and helped determine the conservationist course of action that proved to be his lasting legacy.

In 1933, his first book, *Men of the Last Frontier* was published, and Belenay had begun writing and speaking publically as Grey Owl. The Federal Parks Department took such an interest in Grey Owl's stories that they made a film about his life with the beaver. Jelly Roll, a female beaver who was almost as much of a showman as Grey Owl, starred with him in a display of trust and affection that won the attention of the world.

The story of Grey Owl and the beavers had begun

years before with two orphaned kits named McGinty and McGuinness. The adopted beavers captivated Grey Owl and he became preoccupied with the idea that the beaver was facing extinction. He set his classic childrens' story *Sajo and Her Beaver People* in the great Temagami forest where they lived in a rustic cabin. The tale of native children and two baby beavers remains in print and has been translated into nearly twenty languages.

While he was writing his childrens' book, Grey Owl was also completing his autobiography *Pilgrims of the Wild*, which was published in 1935 by Australian-born Lovat Dickson, who grew up in Canada. Dickson organized a lecture tour for Grey Owl in Britain. At a time when the economies of Canada and England were depressed, Wall Street had crashed, Hitler was mobilizing for war, Mussolini was ranting and raving, and industrial pollution was choking European cities, Grey Owl was a breath of fresh air from an enchanted wilderness. He spoke about forests that had the size and sanctity of medieval cathedrals; about a land where mankind could begin again, where the air was pure and animals roamed free. The crowds loved it. Regardless of the purity of his message, Grey Owl was still a fraud, and for his efforts the consumate con began earning in the princely neighbourhood of $30,000 a year. He drank whiskey almost non-stop on his return crossing. Before he had such an outstanding income, his substance abuse of choice had been vanilla extract.

His final book, *Tales of an Empty Cabin* was published in October 1936 and one month later, tired of being neglected while he incessantly wrote out his stories, Anahereo left Grey Owl. A few weeks later, the much-married and seldom-divorced Archie wed Yvonne Perrier, whose native name was Silver Moon.

A second tour of England and the United States was scheduled for the winter of 1937 through 1938. Once again, Grey Owl was spellbinding, and he looked more "red" than ever, thanks to a sun lamp. He appeared in a command performance for King George, Queen Mary and the Royal Princesses, Elizabeth and Margaret Rose. Eschewing protocol, Grey Owl insisted that all members of his audience be seated before he made his dramatic entry. In his braids, beads and fringed leather costume, the British-born imposter greeted his King in the Ojibway language, which he translated as "I come in peace, brother." Then he showed his films and told his stories. Princess Elizabeth was apparently so enthralled that when it was over she jumped up and cried, "Oh, do go on!" Publisher Lovat Dickson attended the Royal event and notes in his biography *Wilderness Man, The Strange Story of Grey Owl* that, "he was more than ever the Indian, proud, fierce, inscrutable."

Months later, on April 13, 1938, Grey Owl died at his cabin in Prince Albert, Saskatchewan, and the world soon learned that he was a hoax. There was surprise, but no shockwave of disapproval. His masquerade as the Noble Red Man was one of the great thespian performances of the century and his environmental concerns are as relevant today as they were in his lifetime. What better grift than to get away with it in the end.

"EVERY MAN, CARRY A MAN"

Dieppe, France, August 19, 1942 — Honourary Captain John Foote, chaplain of the Royal Hamilton Light Infantry was so determined to accompany his unit into battle that he stowed away with only the tacit consent of his superiors. Then, although he could have left the horror that marked the ill-fated assault on Dieppe, he decided to stay as a prisoner of war!

Foote was a thirty-five-year-old Presbyterian minister in Coburg, Ontario when Canada officially entered the Second World War on September 10, 1939. He was among the earliest to apply for duty and he pursued his duties as a chaplain with his regiment stationed in England. Before the war ended, Canada's forces grew to more than a million men and women from a professional nucleus of fewer than 10,000.

When it became apparent that Canadian troops were to finally be sent into battle on the secret mission dubbed "Operation Jubilee," Foote's commanding officer suggested that the popular padre stay back since he might be needed more than ever after the raid.

"I'll make my own arrangements, and if you see me on the beach you can order me off," replied Foote.

Along with close to 5,000 Canadian troops, Foote joined in the early morning landing at the chalk cliffs off the small port and gambling town of Dieppe. It was the first time most of the men confronted combat, and it was the first time the Allies had determined to test their ability to launch a large-scale amphibious raid on Hitler's continental fortress.

The battle lasted for nine savage hours during which the troops faced incessant, deadly fire. They were raked by machine guns and picked off by snipers. Foote attached himself to a Regimental Aid Post on the beach and set about helping the wounded, constantly exposing himself to the hail of bullets. As the tide went out, the Post moved to a stranded landing craft, and Foote hauled wounded men to its cover, only to remove them when enemy shelling set its ammunition afire.

When evacuation efforts began, the burly padre carried wounded men from the exposed beach to waiting landing craft. "Every man, carry a man," Foote shouted to all who could hear him. He may have saved as many as thirty lives and his courage set an inspirational example.

Foote had several opportunities to embark, but as the last boat departed, he waded back to the bloodied beach. "The men ashore would need me far more in captivity than any of those going home," was his belief.

More than 900 Canadians were killed at Dieppe and nearly 2,000 were taken prisoner. Padre Foote and medical officer Captain D. Clare both chose to be voluntarily imprisoned with the captured men. They led the grim column of captives on the march to prisoner of war camps, where they stayed until the end of the war.

Amid the squalid camp conditions, Foote organized social activities, including an orchestra in which he played a mean trumpet. He conducted regular church services, and also used the church to conceal men who were escaping. Despite threats to his life, the padre harassed the Germans for better treatment for the men.

John Foote was awarded the Victoria Cross for his heroism at Dieppe, as was another brave Canadian, Vancouver's Colonel Charles "Cec" Merritt of the South Saskatchewan Regiment. Of the thousands who served, their valour and courage was singled out but they were not unique. There were many acts of heroism at Dieppe, and many more would follow, each one deserving of the everlasting gratitude of all Canadians.

COURAGE DOWN BELOW

Springhill, Nova Scotia, 1958 — Canada's "singing miner" kept the faith and what faith it was. Maurice Ruddick sang "Happy Birthday" and hymns for eight-and-a-half days to keep the hopes of his fellow miners alive when they were trapped nearly four kilometres underground in the Springhill Mining Disaster. Ruddick was one of the few black miners employed at the Springhill mine. He and 173 other coal miners were just starting their 8:00 to 11:00 evening shift in the Cumberland Pit Shaft Number Two when a small "bump" occurred.

Although the earth may not seem to move beneath our feet, it is constantly shifting. Nowhere is this more apparent than in a mine, where pressure builds up in gaseous pockets causing pressure-releasing shifts called bumps.

An hour after the first bump, a second followed which shook even the surface of the town and created a heart-chilling rumble. It proved to be the most severe bump in North American mining history. Underground, seventy-three were killed instantly by a massive cave-in.

Rescue teams mobilized to find survivors. Within twenty-four hours, more than half of the surviving miners made it to the surface. While anxious family members crowded at the pithead, the fabled team of draegermen who were specially trained to assist in such disasters found themselves hampered by communication breakdowns and ventilation problems.

It seemed to be a miracle when, six days later, a voice was heard through a ventilator pipe that stretched over 8,000 metres below the surface and twelve more miners were saved.

Eight other miners would wait two-and-a-half more days in a metre-high pocket before being discovered in what Maurice Ruddick described as "a dungeon." For one of them, Percy Rector, help would be too late.

As the men waited, wondered and prayed, Ruddick sang. Although the forty-six-year-old father of twelve had suffered a broken leg, the trauma of crawling over fallen bodies to marginal haven, and the stun of toxic gas, he persisted in rallying his comrades' spirits with jokes and tunes.

"I cried quietly in the darkness, but I made sure nobody else heard me. It might have broken the resolve to live," Ruddick admitted in the aftermath.

When the seven men divided their last sandwich and drank the last of their water on November 1st, they also celebrated the birthday of miner Garnet Clarke with a resounding chorus of "Happy Birthday," led by Ruddick. To survive, they chewed moist bark from the pit-wall props, sucked coal, and even drank their own urine.

When the draegermen finally reached them on November 5th, one of the astonished rescuers reported that he found Ruddick "sitting on a stonetack, singing at the top of his lungs."

"Give me a drink of water and I'll sing you a song," he said in greeting, and the long ordeal came to an end.

Ruddick modestly underplayed his inspirational role,

but others felt differently. "If it wasn't for Maurice, they'd have all been dead," the mother of one of the miners told Ruddick's wife. After the disaster, the Springhill mine was closed forever.

The rescue made international headlines and Canada's "singing miner" experienced the spotlight briefly in public tributes. The Governor of Georgia, Marvin Griffin, was so taken with the story that he invited the nineteen Springhill survivors to recuperate on an all-expense-paid holiday at a swank resort. The gracious invitation changed dramatically when the Governor discovered that Ruddick was black. The American south was strictly segregated in those days, and Ruddick's invitation only stood if he agreed to be segregated.

Initially, Ruddick refused the Governor's terms. When it became apparent that his fellow miners planned to refuse to go without him, he accepted the segregated invitation, suggesting to them: "We'll all have our holiday, then we'll be together again." In Georgia, he stayed at one of the few hotels that accepted blacks, while the others stayed at a vacation resort for millionaires. He could not attend functions in their honour, but the men he shared that darkened Springhill tomb with were proud to join a "segregated" celebration for Ruddick.

By popular consensus, Ruddick was named 1958's Canadian Citizen of the Year. When he presented the award to Ruddick, Ontario Premier Leslie Frost described him as "an inspiration to all... a man with the divine attribute of common sense." With the grace of a hero, Ruddick accepted the honour "for every miner in the town."

PART 3

HER STORY

"Desist or I Will Tell Your Wife"

Woman of Wheat

*Canada's Hyena in Petticoats
Lets 'em Howl*

Woman of the House

*She Went Where She Wanted To Go,
Did What She Wanted To Do...*

"You're Not Even a Person"

"DESIST OR I WILL TELL YOUR WIFE"

Toronto, 1871 — When Jennie Trout and Emily Stowe managed to obtain restricted permission to attend a session of lectures at the Toronto School of Medicine, Canadian universities would not allow women to study medicine. In fact, the two women were only allowed to attend on the absolute condition that they agreed "not to make a fuss."

However, the "restricted" sessions were virtually designed to incite a "fuss." With the professors' collusion, their fellow male students jeered the women and took to placing dissected body parts on their chairs. From a hole in the wall between the lecture hall and an anteroom, the aspiring female doctors would check their seats before entering to determine what tricks their classmates had been up to. Obnoxious sketches were drawn on the walls of the lecture room with such frequency that the classroom had to be whitewashed four times during that first semester.

Trout and Stowe endured all this and more. Both were ultimately instrumental in establishing medical colleges for women. The only evidence approaching a "fuss" occurred when one lecturer who persisted in telling sickening and smutty stories, inspired Trout to admonish him to desist or she would advise his wife of exactly what he had said. Apparently, this tactic was effective.

Jennie Trout and Emily Stowe both grew up on Ontario farms. Both excelled in school and went on to become school teachers. At one point, they lived on the same Toronto street. They became friends and shared in discussions of women's rights.

Stowe was a more aggressive personality. In addition to becoming the first Canadian woman to graduate from a medical school, she also founded Canada's first suffrage group, which operated under the title of the Toronto Women's Literary Club for many years.

Trout was ten years younger, and preferred to avoid publicity. Like Stowe, she completed her medical studies in the United States, where medical colleges for women were first established in 1850.

Stowe graduated as a doctor in 1867, and Trout followed eight years later. However, according to an 1869 Act of Parliament, graduates of American colleges could only be licensed to practice in Ontario if they attended a session of Canadian lectures and a matriculation exam.

Emily Stowe chose to ignore the licensing requirements. She practised openly and illegally for thirteen years, and most likely paid the $100 penalty that was levelled for such violation more than once. Although she had qualified in her sessional studies, the feisty Stowe may well have felt that she could not tolerate the second indignity of taking the oral section of the exam before yet another group of hostile men. She was forty-nine when her licence was finally granted in 1880.

Trout, on the other hand, took the exam immediately following her graduation in 1875. As a sign of the times, when her husband picked her up following the oral exam, *he* was complimented on having such a talented and creditably intelligent wife. She became the first Canadian woman to be licensed to practise medicine. However, when she died in 1921 the *Canadian Medical Journal* did not even record the fact.

Emily Stowe and Jennie Trout confronted a system that was designed to thwart their desires to serve the physical needs of all humanity and, using different tactics, they both won.

WOMAN OF WHEAT

Winnipeg, 1898 — When Aunt Alice announced she was "going west" her niece, E. Cora Hind, joined her in the spirit of adventure. Hind had grown up on farms in Flesherton and Orillia, Ontario. She was orphaned early in life and, at the age of twenty-one, she was ready to become a pioneer of sorts.

Hind longed to be a newspaper reporter. The day after her arrival in Winnipeg in 1882, she presented herself to the editor of the *Winnipeg Free Press*. He reportedly was "not interested in skirts" on his reporters, which only stiffened Hind's resolve to one day work for the newspaper.

Early on, Hind displayed a keen eye for trends. When she discovered that no one in Winnipeg knew how to use a typewriter, she promptly rented a machine and mastered the craft, becoming the first typist west of the Great Lakes. With this invaluable skill, she found employment in a law office, bringing her in contact with many land deals, as well as individual farmers. She made it her business to understand what she was typing and conversed knowledgeably with farm clients, who were impressed by the young woman's wide-ranging interest in agriculture.

In 1893 Hind set up her own stenography office. Farm organizations began asking her to report on their meetings and conventions. In those days, wheat prices fluctuated wildly according to the size and quality of the crops. Millers and financiers, along with farmers, were intensely anxious for information. Soon she was preparing reports about agricultural conditions and markets.

Finally, in 1898 she was given her first chance to report on the wheat crop by Colonel J.B. Maclean, founder of Maclean Publications in Toronto. She boarded a train west for Moose Jaw the very night she received his telegram requesting a survey of the fields. This was one of many trains Hind was to take over her long career.

In 1901, she was hired by the *Winnipeg Free Press*. Her knowledge of agriculture rapidly removed her from the "Women's Page," and she was made the paper's agriculture editor. Farmers and businessmen from across the West sent her crop condition reports, but Hind never strayed far from the source for her data. Riding the rails, she questioned everyone she met. Along the way she would stop off at stations, hire a horse and buggy, and journey along the endless prairie roads, climbing a fence now and then to poke the soil to judge its moisture and grab a head of wheat to thresh in her small hand.

Hind's ability to forecast the wheat crop grew to legendary proportions and her reports were telegraphed to markets all over the world. Bankers and grain companies took her estimates as gospel. Her accuracy effected the entire economy.

Her reports were never candy-coated. When she predicted a poor crop, she was nicknamed "Calamity Cora." Her estimate remained unchanged and the official tally showed Hind to be correct. "No one loves the West more than I do," she said, "but very early in my career, I learned that the West was big enough and strong enough to have the truth told about it on all occasions."

When the Canadian Wheat Board took over the task of marketing grain in 1933, it announced that Hind's total of twenty-nine estimates had reflected more accurate forecasting than any government or other official statements.

Hind's love of agriculture was not limited to wheat. She championed Western beef and dairy cattle and served as a director of the Canadian Co-operative Wool Growers. As a livestock judge and as a speaker, she cut a dashing figure wearing her beaded buckskin jacket and odd assortment of hats.

Cora Hind received many honours throughout her career, including a Doctor of Laws degree from the University of Manitoba. She travelled the world, wrote two books about her adventures and spent forty-one years as a reporter.

In 1932, seventy-one-year-old Hind realized a lifelong dream when she accompanied the first cargo of Canadian wheat from Churchill, Manitoba to Great Britain. As the *London Morning Post* reported: "A woman who can go around and look at wheat fields and then come home and estimate the Canadian wheat crop, forecasting it so accurately that bankers and grain companies take her estimate as gospel — such a woman is not met every day."

CANADA'S HYENA IN PETTICOATS LETS 'EM HOWL

Winnipeg, Manitoba, 1916 — What event roused the Manitoba Legislative Assembly to celebrate by singing "For They Are Jolly Good Fellows?" The uncharacteristic outburst was prompted by the passing of a law which granted Manitoba women the right to vote. The political activist who spearheaded the suffrage campaign was Nellie Mooney McClung.

McClung was born in Chatsworth, Ontario and spent most of her childhood in Manitoba where she became a teacher. "Women's roles" fascinated her at an early age, and McClung signed her first petition on behalf of women's suffrage in 1890 at the age of sixteen.

At twenty-three, she married pharmacist Wes McClung and they eventually raised a family of five. During this time, McClung was active in the Women's Christian Temperance Union and she became a popular speaker. She also pursued a writing career, producing her first novel *Sowing Seeds for Danny* in 1908. It became a national best-seller.

After moving to Winnipeg in 1911, McClung became involved in the city's active and vocal women's rights and reform movement. She lobbied Conservative Premier Sir Rodmond Roblin for better working conditions for female factory workers. It was to be her first confrontation with Roblin, but not her last.

In 1914, McClung led a delegation of women to ask for the right to vote. "I don't want a hyena in petticoats talking politics to me. I want a nice gentle creature to bring me my slippers," advised Premier Roblin. The meeting ended when Roblin concluded: "Nice women don't want the vote."

McClung's response was to stage a mock Parliament in which the subject of the debate was whether or not men should have the vote. "Man is made for something higher and better than voting," declared McClung in an excruciatingly humorous and deadly accurate parody of the Premier. "Politics unsettles men, and unsettled men mean unsettled bills — broken furniture, broken vows — divorce."

The mock Parliament was a huge success. Although there was a some public backlash to her rabble-rousing style, as well as vicious attacks by critics who accused her of neglecting her children, McClung maintained her posture through reasonable discussion and irrepressible wit and charm.

"Never retract, never explain, never apologize — get the thing done and let them howl," became McClung's motto. While her critics nicknamed her the "Holy Terror," her supporters and her family cheered her as "Our Nell."

On January 27, 1916, Manitoba's new Liberal government passed the Bill for the Enfranchisement of Women. What McClung had called "a bonny fight, a knockdown drag-out fight, uniting the women of Manitoba in a great cause," was resolved in a victory which paved the way for other provinces and the federal government to determine that women should be granted the vote.

McClung moved to Edmonton, where she continued the struggle for the right to vote in that province. She gained a seat in the Legislature in 1921 and lobbied for everything from free medical and dental treatment for school children to improved property rights for women. Defeat in 1926 did little to curtail her public activities. The following year she became one of the "famous five" who launched the "Persons Case."

"Women are going to form a chain, a greater sisterhood than the world has ever known," said McClung. As an author, lecturer and grandmother, she continued to advocate rights and reforms for women until her death in 1951.

WOMAN OF THE HOUSE

Ottawa, 1922 — Agnes Macphail, Canada's first female Member of Parliament, was chided by the press for failing to wear headgear in the House. In those days, hatlessness was next to political incorrectness. All of Macphail's nineteen years as an Honourable Member were characterized by such unfair derision.

Agnes Macphail was born in a log cabin in Proton Township in Grey County, Ontario near the shores of Georgian Bay in 1890. She was always proud of her rural upbringing, and spent most of her life speaking on behalf of farmers.

After teaching school for several years, Macphail expanded on her rural interests as a member of United Farmers of Ontario. She defeated ten men to become the U.F.O candidate in the 1921 federal election. When losing nominees decided to stir up trouble by asking her to resign and call another convention "in which saner judgement would be possible," Macphail stood her ground. She was thirty-one when she won her first election.

Women had been allowed to vote in federal elections since 1918, but Macphail was the first to take a seat in the House of Commons. Her presence created quite a stir. While many members rose to greet her and welcome her formally in speeches of flowery praise, Macphail discovered that a welcoming bouquet of roses placed on her desk was actually the penance of a man who was paying off an election bet that she would fail.

Outside of the House she was subject to constant staring. The ordeal of eating in the parliamentary restaurant caused such strain that by her own admission she lost twelve pounds during the first session. Above all her recollections of parliamentary initiation were of "a miserable time." In her own words: "Some members resented my intrusion, others jeered at me, while a very few were genuinely glad to see a woman in the House."

The press was of no help. Reporters decided that Macphail was stiff and severe. They preferred analyzing her blue serge suit to the policies she pursued on protective tariffs, her investigation of labour relations and her commitment to penal reform which led to the Archambault Commission.

So hurtful were the attacks, that Macphail ensured that several love letters written to her be stored among her papers for eventual inclusion in the National Archives. She could not bear the thought of being remembered as the stern, frigid spinster the contemporary press made her out to be. In fact, according to Durham, Ontario poet/author Wilma Coutts, who spent her childhood singing at parties in Macphail's riding: "Our Aggie could dance up a storm with the best of them."

She received several marriage proposals, but the institution did not seem to suit her. "One of the outstanding features of this age is the number of intelligent women who do not marry," she noted. "I have talked to hundreds of these fine, alert and very capable women in business, the professions, and the arts, and their reason was the same as mine: *the person* could not be subjected."

Macphail was a "feminist" for her time. She argued for equality and fulfilment for all, with the same vehemence that she argued in favour of world disarmament in a pro-military environment. "When I hear men talk about women being the angel of the home I always, mentally at least, shrug my shoulders in doubt," she told the House during a debate over the Divorce Bill. "I do not want to be the angel of any home; I want for myself what I want for other women, absolute equality. After that is secured then men and women can take turns at being angels."

Macphail remained in the House of Commons until her defeat in 1940. Undaunted, she entered provincial politics, where she sometimes won, and sometimes lost as a member of the C.C.F. Politics was her life.

SHE WENT WHERE SHE WANTED TO GO, DID WHAT SHE WANTED TO DO...

Daniel's Harbour, Newfoundland, 1926 — For more than fifty years, Newfoundland nurse Myra Bennett was the only medical aid along almost 400 kilometres of rugged coastline on the northern peninsula. She set broken limbs, performed kitchen table operations by lamp light and sutured and dressed wounds of every description. Throughout the province she was known as the "Florence Nightingale of the North."

The war-trained, English nurse was twenty-nine when she volunteered for a Newfoundland posting from the British Overseas Nursing Association. She had hoped to be sent to Saskatchewan, a faraway place she read about in a two-penny weekly nursing publication.

Both Lady Grey, wife of Governor General Earl Grey and Lady Harris, wife of Newfoundland Governor Sir Alexander Harris, convinced her that there was a great need for nurses in Newfoundland. In preparation for her new job, the young nurse took a course in midwifery and she acquired some limited tools of her trade, including a device for extracting teeth, a "universal forceps," which was to prove invaluable.

She arrived at Daniel's Harbour in the spring of 1921 and immediately began ministering to everything from difficult childbirths to tuberculosis. Her salary was seventy-five dollars a month, and she worked long hours travelling up and down the coast in all kinds of weather.

In 1922, "Nurse" married Newfoundland sailor and businessman Angus Bennett. He built a large home, which also served as a surgery, education centre and hospital for half a century.

Bennett was three months pregnant with their second child when she received one of her most dramatic calls to duty in the middle of a snowy February night in 1926.

Her brother-in-law, Alex, was working at a lumber camp about eight kilometres from Daniel's Harbour and his foot had been almost completely severed by a saw at the mill. A thin strip of flesh was all that held the foot to the rest of the leg above the exposed ankle joint. Using snow as an anesthetic, Bennett cleaned the foot of splinters and bone and stitched the severed foot back onto the leg as best she could.

The following morning, Myra and Angus set out on a 100 kilometre journey to take the injured man to a doctor at Woody Point. The journey took three days, winding across the ocean on drifting ice and dodging ragged coastal ice. The Bennetts walked beside the sled to make it lighter for the horse as they battled drifting snow, howling winds and exhaustion.

Telegraph wires hummed with news of their journey. They spent the first night at Parson's Pond, where a group of men carried the patient and sled from the ice-encrusted cliffs to a warm home with steaming soup awaiting the weary travellers.

When they finally reached the doctor at Woody Point, he was amazed at Nurse Bennett's handiwork.

There was no need to amputate. After a lengthy recovery, Alex was able to walk again.

Before she retired at sixty-eight, Bennett trained five midwives, raised her own family of three children and fostered four others. She delivered more than 5,000 babies and extracted at least 3,000 teeth in a career that did not end with the formality of retirement. Indeed, the last child she delivered was one of her own grandsons, and she was ninety-two when she performed her final extraction at Daniel's Harbour. "Mum always had strong arms and hands," recalled daughter Barbara Laing of Wawa, Ontario. "Once she got a hold of a tooth, she didn't let go."

Nurse Bennett received the Jubilee Medal from King George V, Coronation medals from both King George VI and Queen Elizabeth II, the Medal of the British Empire, the Order of Canada and an honourary doctorate in science from Memorial University. In 1967, Dr. Bennett was made a life member of the Association of Registered Nurses of Newfoundland in tribute to her "half-century of noble and notable service."

"I went where I wanted to go and I stayed there because I was needed," Myra Bennett once explained. She died in 1990 at the age of 100, leaving a legacy of dedication that honours the best tradition of Canadian nursing.

"You're Not Even a Person"

London, England, 1929 — To say that the fact that women were not considered "persons" in Canada irritated a Canadian magistrate named Emily Ferguson Murphy would be a gross understatement.

The first woman magistrate in the history of the British Empire, Emily Murphy had her legal status as a "person" belligerently challenged on her first day in court in 1916. If that arrogant defense lawyer Eardley Jackson could have imagined the consequences of his challenge, he might have held his tongue. Magistrate Murphy went on to spearhead a thirteen-year effort to change that stupefying state of affairs.

Emily Murphy was born in Cookstown, Ontario in 1868. She was the daughter of well-to-do parents and enjoyed an excellent education. At nineteen, she married an Anglican minister twelve years her senior. They served in parishes throughout Ontario, and spent several years in England. During that time Murphy raised a family of young daughters. She became a journalist and later an author, writing under the pen name "Janey Canuck."

In 1904, the Murphys moved to the Swan River area of Manitoba and then to Edmonton in 1907. In Alberta, Murphy lobbied fiercely for the cause of women's rights and she was instrumental in framing the Dower Act of 1911, which provided property rights for married women.

In 1916, women observers were asked to leave a court session in which a group of prostitutes were being tried. Crown Counsel argued that the evidence would be unsuitable for a mixed audience. This prompted Murphy to argue that the city of Edmonton was in need of a court in which offenders could be tried by women in the presence of women. The Attorney General agreed with her, and promptly appointed Murphy as the first woman Police Magistrate in the Empire.

Murphy found her first day in court "as pleasant an experience as running a rapids." Not surprising, since Eardley Jackson turned on her as she sentenced his bootlegger client.

"You're not even a person," he shouted. "You have no right to be holding court!" Jackson persisted, quoting a statute of British Common Law which stated: "Women are persons in matters of pains and penalties, but are not persons in matters of rights and privileges." Since the position of magistrate was one of "privilege," Jackson concluded that Murphy was sitting "illegally" and no decision of her court could be binding.

In 1917, the Supreme Court of Alberta ruled that as far as it was concerned women were "persons." But the matter did not end there for Murphy, who discovered that according to the British North America Act women were not considered "persons" and as such could not be appointed to the Senate.

On a national scale, women's groups spent years urging the federal government to appoint a woman to the Senate, to no avail. "Whenever I don't know whether to fight or not, I always fight," Murphy once said.

By 1927, Murphy's fighting blood was up. She discovered that under the B.N.A. Act any group of five citizens could petition the Supreme Court of Canada to rule on a constitutional point, and she determined to have an answer to the "person" issue. Four prominent Alberta women joined Murphy in the petition, which became known as the "Persons Case."

When the Supreme Court of Canada ruled that since women held no public office of any kind in 1867, the Fathers of Confederation could have had no intention of including women among the "persons" qualified to be summoned to the Senate, Murphy and her fellow petitioners decided to take their case to the Privy Council in London. Five judges joined a battery of bewigged lawyers from Canada and England in four days of debate over the interpretation of a seven-letter noun.

On October 18, 1929, the decision of the Supreme Court was reversed. Lord Sankey announced that in the view of the Council, the B.N.A. Act had "planted in Canada a living tree capable of growth and expansion." The judgement ruled that "the word person includes members of the female sex," and Sankey noted that: "The exclusion of women from all public offices is a relic of more barbarous times."

Thus, Canadian women were accorded legal status as "persons" and were entitled to sit in the Senate for the first time. If history were devised to construct happy endings, Murphy's supporters would have relished her appointment as the first woman Senator. However, in 1931, Prime Minister Mackenzie King selected a well-known Liberal party worker, Cairine Wilson of Montreal.

Undaunted, Murphy urged women "to rejoice" at the ultimate consequence of their hard-won personhood. She was some kind of a woman.

PART 4
SPORTS

FIELDS OF DREAMS

ROW, ROW, ROW YOUR BOAT

FOLLOW THE BOUNCING BALL

SIMPLY THE BEST

OUR PERCY GOES FOR GOLD

THE COMPLETE ATHLETE

WHO WAS THAT MASKED MAN?

FIELDS OF DREAMS

Oxford County, Ontario, 1838 — Although American Abner Doubleday is often credited with "inventing" baseball in 1839, the fact is that on June 4, 1838, two weeks before Queen Victoria's coronation, and six months after the Mackenzie King Rebellion in Toronto, Canadians played their first recorded game on a smooth pasture behind Enoch Burdick's shops at Beachville, near the southwestern Ontario town of Ingersoll.

Canadian baseball had its origins in English games such as rounders and cricket, which also feature a pitcher, catcher, fielders and batters running to bases. The history of the game is imprecise. Drawings found in Egyptian tombs appear to indicate that a few innings may have been enjoyed by the likes of King Tut, and games utilizing balls and sticks in medieval times often coincided with spring fertility rites.

When the assorted Beachville village players of Oxford County met the neighbouring township team from Zorra, the rules and the implements of the game were slightly different from those we know today. Four bases, called "byes" marked the infield area and eleven players formed a team. The batter was known as a "knocker," while the bat itself was referred to as a "club."

Early bats were fashioned out of cedar, blocked with an axe and finished with a drawing knife. Wagon spokes and barrel staves were also used. The relatively small baseballs were made out of double and twisted woollen yarn covered with calfskin and stitched with waxed thread.

No gloves were worn and the real fun of the game came in "plugging," which involved hitting the runner with a thrown ball. This hazardous practise was revised in the 1860s when a "standard" set of rules was adopted by the Canadian Association of Base Ball Players, and the gentler art of "tagging" the runner for an out came into effect.

Scores were kept on a notched stick and games lasted six to nine innings, or finished when one of the teams achieved a designated number of runs. Hits and runs were numerous, since batters were allowed to wait for their choice of pitches. When the Woodstock Young Canadians played the Atlantic Club of Brooklyn, New York in the first ever international baseball game, their resounding defeat was scored at seventy-five to eleven.

From its small town and rural roots, Canadian baseball evolved as a working-class sport. Players on the first organized team — the Hamilton Young Canadians — included five clerks, three shoemakers, a marble cutter, a tinsmith, a painter and a saloon-keeper, along with makers of everything from brooms to carriages.

Although players were praised for their "gentlemanly bearing," games between communities became heated affairs and fights in the bleachers were not uncommon. The popularity of the game was confirmed in 1869, when the town of Woodstock hosted a three-day tournament and attracted 5,000 spectators, which was at least 1,000 in excess of the southwestern Ontario town's entire population.

In 1876 the Canadian Base Ball Association was formed. It featured a five-team league, including the London Tecumsehs who went on to defeat the National League champion Chicago White Stockings in an exhibition match. The following year the Tecumsehs defeated Pittsburgh to become champions of the National League's principal rival organization, the International Association.

Baseball fever spread across Canada. Games with U.S. teams were prevalent in Victoria and New Westminster, B.C. By the mid-1880s, inter-town matches were played in New Brunswick. In Manitoba, Winnipeggers were said to be suffering from "baseball mania" and open gambling on the games raised public concern.

Canadians, such as players George "Moon" Gibson and James Edward "Tip" O'Neil and managers Arthur Irwin and Bill Watkins, went on to enjoy substantial professional careers in the United States as part of the first "foreign invasion" of the game in America.

Although the vast majority of professional league players in Canada were recruited from the United States, by 1900 baseball was the most popular and most publicized sport in the country.

The imagination of Canadians has been seized in the field of dreams ever since.

ROW, ROW, ROW YOUR BOAT

Paris, France, 1867 — Three fishermen, and a lighthouse keeper — that was the "Paris Crew." Believe it or not, this ragtag rowing team from St. John, New Brunswick won the prestigious Paris Regatta in 1867. Just weeks after Confederation, they became a newborn nation's first world-champions.

"With their flesh-coloured jerseys, dark cloth trousers, leather braces and bright pink caps, they were in striking contrast to their neat competition," was how the *Manchester Guardian* euphemistically understated the spectacle these rough-hewn, freshly-minted Canadians presented at this most elite of events.

But it was not only the appearance of Elijah Ross, the lighthouse keeper, and fishermen Robert Fulton, George Price and Samuel Hutton that struck an odd chord. Instead of the sleek shells that were used by the likes of the Oxford Blues rowing team and the French Geslings, the Paris Crew had two, home-made, lime green boats that weighed a good fifty kilograms more than those of their competitors.

Furthermore, the Canadians had the audacity to argue publicly amongst themselves, which did not sit well in "civilized" rowing circles. Reporters balked at their short-stroke rowing style — "by no means in accordance with received ideas." And to defy convention even further, they chose to compete without a coxswain, the diminutive individual who traditionally provides instructions from the bow of the boat. Reception, perception and eccentricities aside, the Paris Crew had the unwavering support of their countrymen. To send the foursome to Paris, the citizens of St. John raised $4,000 and the provincial government subscribed another $2,000. These were staggering sums of money in those days, but the vigour of gambling potential may have spurred the goodwill.

Sheriff Harding of St. John accompanied the rowers to the "sinful" city to protect the "investment" and to levy tens of thousands of dollars in wagers on behalf of his constituency.

The Crew was entered in two races, one for heavy in-rigged boats and the other for out-rigged shells.

They triumphed in both!

According to one English description of the first race: "The Canadians were not supposed to have a chance... Yet they won by three lengths with London second and Oxford third. At the finish, they were ploughing away, clear of the others, laughing and talking in the easiest possible manner."

The victories became a national inspiration to the new country. "Perhaps nothing since Confederation has occurred which so thoroughly brings home to the broad mass of our people that our bold Maritime friends are now our fellow countrymen in name and in fact," noted *The Toronto Globe*.

In 1868, the fabulous four did it again, and beat the best America had to offer. They appeared indomitable. During a race against a Toronto crew, the New Brunswickers were so far ahead that they paused to share a bottle of wine and still won their race.

When the Paris Crew was surprised by defeat at the 1870 Lachine Regatta in Quebec, St. Johners demanded a rematch against the victorious team from Tyne, which was stroked by the great English single sculls champion James Renforth.

The race was scheduled for August 23, 1871 over 9.7 kilometres of the Kennebecasis River, just east of St. John. Race day was declared a public holiday and a crowd of more than 20,000 celebrated. In those days rowing was such a huge spectator sport that throngs gathered just to observe the team practise.

The Paris Crew, stripped to the waist and rowing at forty-two strokes a minute, had taken a commanding lead when the English boat suddenly veered off course. Renforth had collapsed. Shortly afterward, the twenty-nine-year-old champion was dead.

Confusion reigned. Rumours spread, with some accounts suggesting that Renforth's last words had been: "Oh Harry, I've had something." English newshounds rushed to the conclusion of murder most foul — by poison!

At the inquest that followed, medical experts in Boston absolved the good citizens of St. John. No poison was found. The cause of death has been cited variously as either heart failure or asphyxia, attributed to congestion in the lungs brought on by mental and physical stress.

Later, in tribute to the fallen rower, a town at the river's edge was named Renforth. But after the tragedy, the Paris Crew never raced again. No one would accept their challenge, and the St. John Four went into rather ignominious retirement.

Nine years later, in 1880, Canada earned its second world championship, when Toronto oarsman Edward "Ned" Hanlan beat Australia's Edward Tickett in a race viewed by more than 100,000 spectators on the River Thames in England.

In 1984, Canada's rowers earned gold at the Olympics and, after the success of our rowers in the 1992 Barcelona Summer Olympics, there can be no doubt that our nation is blessed with a tradition of golden oars.

FOLLOW THE BOUNCING BALL

Springfield, Massachusetts, 1891 — It all started with two peach baskets, a soccer ball and a few Americans. They wanted to call it "Naismith ball." Typical of many Canadians, James Naismith was too modest to allow them to name a game after him. So they called it "basketball" instead.

This most American of sports, and now the world's most widely played game, was indeed invented by a young physical education teacher from Almonte, Ontario.

Very few sports have actually been "invented." Hockey, another uniquely Canadian game, evolved from the native peoples' fast-paced game of lacrosse. Football is a rugby derivative.

James Naismith, a doctoral graduate in theology from McGill University and Presbyterian Theological College in Montreal, practised his faith in the belief that a healthy mind was inseparable from a healthy body.

In 1891, Naismith found himself in charge of a bored and rebellious gym class made up of mature men at the YMCA training school in Springfield, Massachusetts. Where other instructors had failed, he was determined to discover an indoor sport that would fill the gap between the football and baseball seasons.

"All of the stubbornness of my Scottish ancestry was aroused, all of my pride of achievement urged me on," he once recalled.

Naismith tried modifying traditional games, but tackling and full-bore running proved hazardous on the hard gymnasium floor. One by one, Naismith thought out the elements of the new game.

He recalled a childhood game that involved knocking a rock off another rock with a stone.

He also remembered an off-season rugby exercise he had practised at McGill that involved throwing a ball into an empty box at the end of a gymnasium.

Why not elevate the goals? A soccer ball was light enough to be thrown and caught. To make the goals, he borrowed two peach baskets from the janitor.

On December 21, 1891, he posted thirteen rules on the YMCA bulletin board.

When the men came by to wile away a few hours with the intense but likable doctor of divinity, they found that all the traditional gym apparatus had disappeared.

Rings and climbing ropes were slung out of the way to clear "air space" over the sloped peach baskets that were nailed to the balconies at either end of the room.

At first, the men were sceptical. One may even have had the audacity to ask: "Is this some kind of Canadian joke?"

Early games must have been amusing to watch. The traditional gym uniforms of the day consisted of long grey trousers and short-sleeved jerseys, worn by players who favoured full beards or walrus moustaches.

In the beginning, there were nine competitors on each team. When a player was cornered too closely to throw, he would roll the ball and run after it. The first game of basketball ever played ended in a score of one to zero, a far cry from the NBA scores of today.

As the game caught on, refinements were made; the skill level increased and the "dribble" was introduced. However, the janitor quickly grew tired of climbing up and down a ladder to retrieve the soccer ball from the peach baskets.

"Let's cut the bottom out of the baskets," Naismith declared and the "hoop" as we know it took shape at each end of the "court."

Although his students preferred "Naismith ball" as a title, the inventor just laughed. "I told them I thought *that* name would kill any game." A student came up with "basketball."

A truly egalitarian sport, basketball stresses skill over strength, speed and power. The same sport that is played in $200 spring-loaded sneakers and satin shorts is also played in wheelchairs.

James Naismith, a man from a country where the climate forces its population indoors half the year, invented a pastime that has become one of the most popular sports in the history of human endeavour.

SIMPLY THE BEST

Edmonton, 1915 — In the history of sport there has never been anything like Alberta's legendary Edmonton Commercial Graduates women's basketball team. The statistics speak for themselves: they won ninety-six percent of their games, held the title of "World Champions" for seventeen consecutive years and had a winning streak that lasted for 147 consecutive games. Scarcely a generation after James Naismith invented the game, his countrywomen formed a team that many contend was "simply the best."

"They are champions because they are the most whole-hearted, sport-loving girls that it would be possible to find," said the man who served the Grads as both teacher and coach. "They have won because the spirit of the Prairies is born and bred in them."

Basketball had evolved considerably from its peach basket beginnings, when Percy Page introduced the game to his girl's physical education class at Edmonton Commercial High School in 1914. Enthusiasm ran high when the school team won their first city title.

In 1915, Page organized a senior team which combined the talents of students and former students who wanted to continue playing. In their first season the Grads won the Alberta title, and they held onto it for twenty-four out of the next twenty-five years.

Their horizons broadened in 1922, when the first Canadian women's basketball championships were held in London, Ontario. Once again the Grads won on their first try. They retained the title for eighteen years.

The Underwood Typewriter Company put up a challenge cup in 1923, which was tantamount to the women's world championships since it involved teams from all provinces and every state. The Edmonton Grads never lost a series. When the team disbanded in 1940, the Underwood Trophy was awarded to its only winner.

The Grads had an uncanny cohesion and coach Page ran a tight ship, establishing a "farm system" that gradually moved players from high school basketball positions onto the Gradettes, and finally the Grads.

Page insisted on the importance of physical conditioning — two practises weekly during the season, and no drinking or smoking. "You must play basketball, think basketball and dream basketball," he told his players, and they rewarded him with complete loyalty, and dazzling shooting skills.

"He's a perfect dear, but we don't have to do a thing he tells us unless we like," one of the Grads once remarked.

Wherever they played the Grads drew big crowds. Over the years they travelled more than 200,000 kilometres, attending four Olympic-related competitions in Paris, Amsterdam, Los Angeles and Berlin.

Unfortunately for Canada, basketball did not become a sanctioned event until 1976. In their exhibition matches at the 1924, 1928, 1932 and 1936 Olympic Games, the Grads never lost a match and they out-scored their opponents a remarkable 1,863 points to 297.

The team financed itself from gate proceeds, but the players never received a penny. Their only motivation was a love of basketball. When the all-time high-scorer, Noel MacDonald, was inducted into the Canadian Sports Hall of Fame in 1971, she admitted that she was "not altogether comfortable" at being singled out. "We were a team," she said. "We were closer than sisters."

As part of the war effort, the team's playing facility was appropriated by the Royal Canadian Air Force in 1940. The Edmonton Grads disbanded — every one of them a winner.

Percy Page went into politics and ended up becoming the Lieutenant Governor of Alberta in 1959.

James Naismith was a long-time fan of the Grads. He called them "the finest basketball team that ever stepped out on a floor."

The Grads took their compliments with grace. In everyday life they were filing clerks, stenographers and school teachers. When alumnus Winnie Martin was asked if she thought Naismith would have changed the game in any way after seeing the Grads play, she responded: "I think it's obvious. He'd have put the basket higher."

OUR PERCY GOES FOR GOLD

Amsterdam, 1928 — Few Canadians had heard of Vancouver's Percy Williams when he crouched in the blocks preparing to sprint against the best runners in the world at the 1928 Olympics in Amsterdam. His double victory in the 100 and 200 metres track events stunned the world. In 1964, Saskatchewan's Harry Jerome would flash for silver in the 100 metre and Ontario's Ben Johnson would lose a gold in the sports humiliation of the 1988 Games, but Williams took home the ultimate prize in both of his events.

Percy Williams was an unlikely Olympian. He suffered from a damaged heart as a result of childhood rheumatic fever and he had no all-consuming ambition to be a runner. When his coach, Bob Granger, first spotted Williams at a high school meet in 1926 he described him as "a puny 110-pound [50 kilogram] kid."

Nevertheless, Granger saw the spark of talent. When he took Williams under his wing it was with the express resolve to win Olympic gold in 1928. The coach had theories about training and conditioning to go with his vast experience. The modest protégé took instruction without questioning.

Modern coaches might well question some of Granger's techniques. He made Williams give up swimming because he felt it affected his speed, and instead of gruelling regimens Granger believed in conserving energy. For example, it has been reported that on a cold day before a race, Granger would dress Williams' body with coconut butter and force him to wear layers of track suits and sweaters to conserve body heat.

Williams ran most of his races in British Columbia, and by the spring of 1928 he was clocking some remarkable times for a schoolboy. When he went east to compete in the Canadian Olympic trials at Hamilton, Ontario in 1928, he won the 200 metre race. His victory in the 100 metres equalled the 10.6 second Olympic record of the day.

Still, only Granger believed that Williams had a chance against the best in the world. When the Canadian Olympic Committee refused to pay his passage to Holland, Granger worked his way across the Atlantic on a cattle boat, arriving three days after the team.

Williams was drilled in technique right up to the eve of the races. In his hotel room, Granger piled a mattress against one wall and rehearsed starting procedures, sending the now fifty-five kilogram Williams bursting across the room into the bedding.

The practise paid off on July 30th. The unknown underdog shot off the blocks leaving five world-class runners behind him for the entire 100 metres. The stadium erupted. Canadian Olympic chairman P.J Mulqueen rushed onto the field and kissed Williams, whose first words after the race were said to be: "Won't Granger be pleased."

Two days later, the focused Canadian won the 200 metres in a driving finish. General Douglas MacArthur, then the president of the U.S. Olympic Committee, declared Williams "the greatest sprinter the world has ever known."

Williams' triumphant return was celebrated across the country. In Vancouver, school was let out for the day. Before a cheering throng, Mayor Louis Taylor presented Williams with a sports car and Granger with $500 in gold. The favoured snack of the day became the Our Percy chocolate bar.

In the following two years, Williams defeated all of the great American sprinters. He set world records of 4.9 seconds in the forty-five-yard dash and 10.3 seconds for the 100-metres.

On August 23, 1930, during the 100-yard final at the British Empire Games in Hamilton, Williams pulled a muscle in his left thigh. Although he won the race, the injured leg was never right again. He failed to qualify in either of his specialties at the 1932 Olympics.

The slim and unassuming young man who had come out of nowhere to beat the established athletes of the world, quietly dropped out of competitive sport and devoted himself to a business career in Vancouver.

With the glory behind him, Williams admitted no regrets in a 1954 interview. "I was simply bewildered by it all," he said. "I didn't like running. I was so glad to get out of it all."

THE COMPLETE ATHLETE

Amsterdam, 1928 —She won Olympic gold in 1928 and was named Canadian Woman Athlete of the Half-Century, but little Fanny Rosenfeld never had a coach. Popularly known as "Bobbie," she has been described as "the complete athlete." In fact, her biographers suggest that the most efficient way to summarize her career is to say that she was *not* proficient at swimming. In hockey, baseball, basketball, tennis and track and field, Rosenfeld was a champion.

She was born in 1903 in Russia and came to Barrie, Ontario as an infant with her parents. Early on she attracted the attention of the sporting establishment when she beat the reigning Canadian 100-yard champion, Rosa Grosse, at a small track meet in Beaverton, Ontario. Later, Rosenfeld and Grosse shared the world record for 100 yards at eleven seconds flat.

In 1922, Rosenfeld moved to Toronto and entered active competition. Constance Hennessey, one of the founding members of the Toronto Ladies Athletic Club, recalled the determination of the diminutive Rosenfeld.

"She did not look powerful, but she was wiry and quick. Above all she went after everything with full force."

Although hockey was her first love, Rosenfeld's prowess was multi-dimensional. In 1924, she won the Toronto grass court tennis championship and throughout the 1920s she played on several Ontario and eastern Canadian championship basketball teams.

In 1925, her "club" won the points title at the Ontario Track and Field Meet, with firsts in the discus, the 220 yards, the 120-yard low hurdles and seconds in the javelin and the 100-yard dash. This was particularly impressive since the "club," which was sponsored by the chocolate factory where Rosenfeld worked, had only one "member" — Bobbie Rosenfeld.

Rosenfeld established Canadian records in the long jump, standing broad jump and the discus which stood until the 1950s. Wearing her brother's teeshirt and swim trunks, and her father's socks, she thrilled 5,000 spectators at the Olympic Trials in Halifax. She was a character, and the people loved her.

The Amsterdam Olympics of 1928 marked the first time women were admitted to track and field competition — overcoming arguments that vigorous physical activity would damage female reproductive organs and was "unseemly."

The Ninth Olympiad was the highlight of Bobbie Rosenfeld's career. As the anchor runner in the four-member, 400-metre relay team, Rosenfeld brought home a gold. Photographers could barely capture a picture of the exhuberant Canadian team, as the women celebrated in a whirl of exhilarated motion.

The 100-yard dash was another matter. Three Canadians faced two Germans and an American. Tension was high, and Rosenfeld's undefeated team-mate, Myrtle Cook, was disqualified after two false starts, as was one of the German competitors. The race was over in 12.5 seconds and witnesses suggested that Rosenfeld was robbed of a gold in a tight finish that placed her second to the American runner.

Ultimately, it may be her fifth place finish in the 800 metres that shows the true mettle that Bobbie Rosenfeld was made from. Although she had not trained at that distance, Rosenfeld was entered to encourage seventeen-year-old team-mate, Jean Thompson. From ninth position, the more mature runner watched as the teenager began to falter, and she moved up to coax her on. Then, as team manager Alexandrine Gibb noted: "She refused to go ahead of the youngster." Thompson took fourth. Rosenfeld had quietly demonstrated the generous spirit of a champion.

Less than a year later, she was stricken with arthritis. Although bed-ridden for eight months and on crutches for a year, in 1931 she was back as the leading home-run hitter in a major softball league. The following winter, she was the outstanding player in Ontario women's hockey.

In 1932, Rosenfeld coached the Canadian women's track team at the British Empire Games. Arthritis forced her to retire from active sports in 1933. She became one of the first inductees to the Canadian Sports Hall of Fame in 1949. In the same year, a Canadian Press poll named her Woman Athlete of the Half-Century.

Rosenfeld blazed many trails. For over twenty years she wrote a sports column in *The Globe and Mail*, covering everything from horse-racing to wrestling with an irreverent humour. When she died in 1969, the newspaper paid tribute to her as "that rarity, a natural athlete."

WHO WAS THAT MASKED MAN?

New York, New York, November 1, 1959 — Although it looked like something out of a Stephen King nightmare, there came a time when Jacques Plante would not step near a goal crease without his home-made face mask. The immortal Montreal Canadiens' goalie's invention literally changed the face of hockey.

Plante was a player who dared to be different. Wearing protective headgear went against all of the game's "macho" traditions. He also had a habit of knitting in the dressing room before games.

As the oldest of eleven children in a Shawinigan, Quebec family during the Depression, his youthful education included learning to cook and sew and make his own sweaters.

A sports columnist recalled seeing twenty-two-year-old Plante wearing a toque and jersey of his own creation when he was playing with the Montreal Royals. Plante continued to knit throughout his career, contending that it helped him relax and refine his supple hands.

Throughout his career Plante was considered something of an eccentric and a loner. Some suggested that he was a hypochondriac. In fact, he suffered from asthma. To avoid smoke-filled rooms, he would often divorce himself from the team, especially when they were on the road.

He was not one to mince words, particularly on the topic of the stress of goalkeeping. "How would you like it, if you were doing your job in an office and you made a little mistake?" he once asked. "Suddenly a bright light flashed on, a loud buzzer went off, and 18,000 people started screaming: 'Get the bum out of there!'"

On the ice, Plante was a study in focus. When a teammate scored on him in practice, he would stare straight ahead as though the puck had not gone in.

Plante revolutionized the net minder's position by pioneering the move behind the net to stop the puck and leaving it for a defenceman or passing it off to a teammate along the boards. His risky style outside of the "cage" unsettled coaches and drove fans to distraction. The press nicknamed him "Jake the Snake."

Goaltenders of that era often suffered from the pressure of "seeing too much rubber," a sporting euphemism for laceration, concussion and general contusion caused by the repetitious collision of speeding pucks and goal tenders' skulls. Plante finally saw too much "rubber" during a game at Madison Square Gardens on November 1, 1959, when a powerful shot by the New York Rangers' Andy Bathgate redefined his profile, inflicting a deep gash that took seven stitches to close.

After receiving a total of 200 previous stitches in the face, Plante decided he had paid his dues to the gods of the national sport and stubbornly held his own against Canadiens' coach Toe Blake, who believed a player had to "fight for his life" to play well.

That night, with his face sewn from nose to lip, Plante agreed to return to the ice only if he was allowed to wear the home-made face mask he had been wearing in practises since 1955.

This cream-coloured mask drew a mixture of criticism, admiration and wisecracks. Nevertheless, the team went on to win the game four to one.

To keep his mask, which he was supposed to give up once he healed, Plante outdid himself by leading an eleven-game winning streak. The Canadiens won the Stanley Cup the following spring.

With a keen sense of showmanship, Plante appeared in public wearing a plastic or fibreglass mask looking like something from a Frankenstein film. And he made the masks as well.

Overall, he produced several models for himself and fellow players, constantly improving their strength, visibility and lightness. In the 1960s and 1970s, protective face masks with captivating graphics flourished in the NHL and were even the subject of art exhibitions.

Today, the goalie face mask is mandatory gear for anyone courageous and agile enough to assume that critical place in the game.

Jacques Plante's playing career spanned two decades, during which he won the prestigious Vezina Trophy seven times. His legacy is part of hockey's history, and his "moves" are imitated by players from pee wee to professional in the game that formally became Canada's national winter sport in 1994.

PART 5
ART & ARTISTS

MARCHING THUNDER

St. Hyacinthe, Quebec, 1834 — Who has tamed the wind? Joseph Casavant was born in 1807 and he apprenticed as a blacksmith in his adolescence. Although he became known as a skilled craftsman, Casavant maintained a passion for music and dreamed of a career as a musician.

At twenty-seven, he shut down his forge to pursue a classical education. It was a bold move for a man of his age. Casavant enrolled in a seminary, where he worked as a handyman to pay for his studies.

His perseverance was rewarded when the seminary director asked him to repair an organ. A whole world suddenly opened up for the musical blacksmith. Relying on a scholarly work by a French Benedictine monk, Casavant proceeded to disassemble and rebuild the organ. Applying his blacksmith skills, he fashioned and refined its delicate and precise mechanisms.

Casavant called the completed organ "Marching Thunder." It was such a success that a nearby parish ordered one. The "wind tamer" from St. Hyacinthe had found a second career.

Between 1840 and 1866, Casavant completed seventeen instruments which found homes in cities and towns throughout Upper and Lower Canada. The organ that he built for the cathedral in Bytown (now Ottawa) in 1850 was the largest in North America. It consisted of 1,063 wooden and metal pipes, eighteen five-octave stops and a three-keyboard console. Sadly, none of Casavant's original masterpieces remain. However, his sons, Joseph-Claver and Samuel-Marie, inherited his love of the instrument. They studied its science and traditions in Europe.

In 1879, Casavant's sons opened an organ manufacturing workshop at the site of their father's studio. Their first commission was for the organs at Montreal's Notre-Dame Church. This triumph of tonality established their reputation.

By the turn of the century just about every city and town in Canada had a Casavant organ, and the company's reputation spread throughout the world. A wind instrument manufactured in Canada since 1834 now earned an international reputation for excellence.

More than 3,700 organs have been meticulously crafted at Casavant Fréres studio in St. Hyacinthe near Montreal, and the inspiration for this thriving family business came from the musical aspirations of a village blacksmith. Today, ninety percent of the company's production is exported.

While the Casavant family's enterprising passion for excellence in large-scale organs has resulted in an on-going business, another Canadian organ innovator, Frank Morse Robb, was not so fortunate.

Robb was the inventor of the first electronic wave organ ever manufactured. In 1927, he began experimenting with recording the natural wave form of sound on the Bridge Street United Church in Belleville, Ontario. In 1928, Robb obtained a Canadian patent, seven years before any other electronic organs were produced.

Rather than sell his idea, Robb set up his own company. By 1936 the Robb Wave Organ Company was delivering organs to stores and chapels in Toronto, but the Depression spelled doom for Robb's entrepreneurial venture.

The company folded the following year, but the multiplicity of sounds that can be orchestrated on the electronic organ continue to delight millions who can share the thrill of "marching thunder" in their own homes.

WANDERINGS OF AN ARTIST

Hudson's Bay Company Territory, 1846 — Artists have never been known for business acumen or their ability to deal with the mundane details of daily life and Paul Kane, one of Canada's greatest painters, was no exception.

Kane began his career applying his painterly talents on household goods and signs in Coburg, Ontario. He also almost missed the boat on the expedition to the West that resulted in the largest body of his work.

Kane was born in Ireland in 1810. The family immigrated to the village of York (now Toronto) in 1819 and Kane studied art at Upper Canada College. After practising his craft in the trades, he spent nine years roaming the United States and Europe, painting portraits and studying the works of the great masters.

In London, Kane met American painter George Catlin who was exhibiting his paintings of the prairies and foothills of the Rockies. Catlin told Kane that North American artists had a duty to record the cultures of the native peoples before they were lost to posterity.

Kane made Catlin's remarks his creed, and he returned to Canada absorbed in his dream of "devoting whatever talents and proficiency I possess to the painting of a series of pictures illustrative of the North American Indians and scenery."

He spent the summer of 1845 visiting and sketching the Great Lakes tribes. Westward travel was made possible by Sir George Simpson, the "Little Emperor" of the Hudson's Bay Company which held the whole territory west of the Lakehead under charter and licence. Simpson was so impressed by the artist and his goal that he commissoned about a dozen paintings and put in a special request for Kane to capture the annual buffalo hunt.

In the spring of 1846, Paul Kane set out to join the fur brigade with Simpson's personal letter of introduction instructing that he receive "kind attentions and hospitalities and passage from post to post free of charge."

Kane's mettle was soon challenged when he missed a steamboat at Mackinac. He hired a small skiff with a blanket for a sail and managed to catch up with the Company team.

The whole trip was an adventure of epic proportion. Kane witnessed the annual buffalo hunt at the Red River Settlement. He even participated and apparently bagged two of the mighty beasts in a flurry of killing that involved a herd of four to five thousand. Later, he survived the attack of a grizzly bear and crossed the Rocky Mountains on snowshoes.

Kane followed the Columbia River to its mouth. On Vancouver Island he sketched the northern native people, including the Haida. He encountered a gathering of 1,500 warriors of the Blackfoot nation and documented their horse races, dances and rituals.

The journey ended in 1848 and Kane spent the next decade in Toronto translating approximately 700 sketches into enormous canvases. Critics tend to prefer the immediacy and authenticity of the sketches to the larger works, which reflect Kane's European influences and perpetuate the European myth of the Noble Savage. However, in his portraits of native chiefs and ceremonies, Kane clearly captures the strength of his subjects, providing historical detail which has a photographic quality.

Along with his legacy of art, Kane also published the diary of his travels. *Wanderings of an Artist among the Indians of North America* was translated into French, German and Danish and became a best-seller.

Paul Kane died in 1871, his eyesight gone, his dream achieved.

CANADA'S NATIONAL CONTRAPUNTAL CANTATA

Quebec City, June 24, 1880 — "Chant National" — the rousing cantata of contrapuntal orchestration composed by Calixa Lavallée was written in Quebec a century before it became "O Canada."

Although it was approved as our national anthem in 1967 and was designated officially by the National Anthem Act of Parliament in 1980, the song was introduced in Quebec City on June 24, 1880. It was not heard in English Canada until the turn of the century, when lyrics by Montreal-based lawyer and author Robert Stanley Weir were adopted.

In January 1880, Quebec City organizers began planning a dazzling celebration to which St. Jean Baptiste Societies in Canada and the United States were invited. The music committee boosted enthusiasm when it proposed the inclusion of a national song in the program. Reportedly, the Governor General had composed a poem called "Dominion Hymn" and asked British composer, Sir Arthur Sullivan, to set it to music as a national anthem.

This apparently riled the St. Jean Baptiste Society and they determined a counter-offering.

The words of a poem written for the occasion by Judge Adolphe-Basile Routhier were selected and Lavallée was commissioned to compose the music.

Calixa Lavallée was a pioneer in music, both in Canada and the U.S. He was born in Vercheres, Lower Canada in 1842 and his first musical studies were with his father. When he was barely a teenager he left Canada for the U.S. and toured throughout South America, the West Indies and Mexico. The year following his return to Vercheres, the twenty-one-year-old musician and teacher gave a concert in Montreal playing piano, violin and cornet.

Lavallée orchestrated a tour de force for the St. Jean Baptiste celebrations, which began with a huge crowd which assembled to attend ceremonial Mass on the Plains of Abraham.

Throughout the day, a parade moved through the main streets of Quebec City featuring a hundred or so French Canadian societies and associations, preceded by their marching bands and allegorical floats, along with participants from neighbouring American states.

In the evening, an assembly of 3,000 vocalists and musicians performed a programme of appropriately stirring works, leading to Lavallée's mighty climax with a composition that has been equated to a simultaneous rendition of "God Save the Queen," "Vive La Canadienne" and "Coming Through the Rye."

To an awed public silence, conductor Joseph Vezina led three bands in a rousing rendition of Lavallée's "Chant." The song won the hearts of French Canadians, and the approval of the guests of honour — Governor General Lord Lorne and his wife Princess Louise, Queen Victoria's daughter.

With a fresh triumph in hand, Lavallée then found himself several hundred dollars out of pocket, since the civic committee that had retained him reported with regret that it did not have the funds to pay him and the musicians.

Such luck seemed to permeate the composer's career. For example, an opera he had written in Boston was cancelled when the owner of the opera house was murdered!

Lavallée's musical accomplishments have survived him in compositions such as "Le Papillon" and his comic opera *The Widow*. However, in the hearts of Canadians the greatest legacy of the maestro can be felt in the choke of pride that swells whenever "O Canada" is played throughout our home and native land and around the world.

THE WRECK OF THE MARCO POLO

Cavendish Beach, Prince Edward Island, 1883 — Did the explorer Marco Polo ever visit the Cavendish coast of Prince Edward Island? The question is fanciful, although the residents of the red sand beach-front may have spread such a rumour at the turn of the century.

The only "Marco Polo" known to have landed at Prince Edward Island is a three-masted, three-deck sailing vessel that ran aground within sight of land on the morning of July 25, 1883.

The *Marco Polo* was built at St. John, New Brunswick in 1851 and in her day she was known as the fastest merchant ship in the world. The 156 metre, 1,475 tonne ship resembled a cross between a cargo ship and a yacht. One observer suggested she carried "the belly of an alderman on the legs of a ballet dancer."

Her spring launch may have portended her future, since the *Marco Polo* ended up jammed in the mud, and eventually capsized in the ebbing tide. Naval experts speculate that the mud may have re-shaped her hull in some way, which could account for her legendary speed. Once she had been dug out, the *Marco Polo* crossed the Atlantic in just sixteen days.

The Black Ball Line of Australia bought the clipper and refitted her as a luxury passenger vessel. On her first voyage from Liverpool to Australia she accomplished a record outward run of sixty-eight days and round trip record of five months and twenty-one days.

For a decade, the *Marco Polo* maintained a distinguished career. Then, in 1861, she hit an iceberg on the homeward journey and had to limp to the Chilean port of Valparaiso for repairs.

By 1867, the once proud *Marco Polo* had become a tramp transport vessel under the Norwegian flag. Her final cargo was a load of pine lumber.

There are divided opinions about the cause of the wreck of the *Marco Polo*. Insurance fraud was contended, since the ship was in unprofitably poor repair. Alternately, foul wind and weather, compounded by leaking that the inboard pumps failed to stem, may have led the captain to run her ashore to save his crew and cargo.

The arrival of the wreck's twenty crew members — a colourful lot of Irish, English, Scots, Spaniards, Dutch, Germans and Tahitians — created quite a stir in Cavendish. Dignitaries from the Norwegian government, insurance adjustors and surveyors all came to examine the stranded ship.

One week later, others came from as far away as Quebec, St. John, Sackville, Moncton, Shediac and Kouchibouguac, New Brunswick to take part in the auction of anything and everything that remained of the *Marco Polo*. The sale raised the princely sum of $8,000 and many local residents clamoured to bid on any small item bearing the name of the ship.

One observer to the wreck of the *Marco Polo* was an eight-year-old Cavendish girl, who carefully noted the details of the tragedy and the personalities involved. Seven years later she translated her recollections in an essay titled: "The Wreck of the *Marco Polo*." It won third prize in the Queen's County division of the Canada Prize Competition of 1890. The following year, the stirring eyewitness account was published in the Montreal *Witness*. It was the first major newspaper story published by its author. Her name was Lucy Maud Montgomery and she went on to write *Anne of Green Gables*.

THE DIVA OF THE SACRED FIRE

Montreal, 1883 — In Venice, flowers were tossed in the path of her gondola. In Africa, a Zulu warrior wearing a grass G-string asked her to sing her theme song "Home Sweet Home." The Czar of Russia presented her with a diamond-encrusted cross and Queen Victoria gave her pearls. Soprano Emma Albani was Canada's first international star, but she never abandoned her French-Canadian roots. Her triumphant return to the province of her birth in 1883 was greeted by 10,000 admirers. Poet Louis-Honoré Frechette dedicated a poem to her, and she was paraded through the wintry streets in a handsome carriage preceded by the band of the Sixty-Fifth Regiment and followed by a boisterous honour guard of snowshoers setting off firecrackers.

Albani was born in 1847 at Chambly near Montreal, where she was baptized Marie-Louise-Cécile-Emma Lajeunesse. When she was a toddler her mother began giving her piano lessons. At five, her father, a professional music teacher, took over. She practised four hours a day in a training program that included lessons in piano, harp and singing.

Following her mother's death, Emma and her younger sister, Cornelia, were enrolled at a prestigious Montreal convent school, where their father obtained a teaching position and free education for his daughters. The young woman's vocal skill was quickly recognized as advanced for her years. One reviewer described it as "a voice that seemed sent from heaven."

When she was barely a teenager, Emma performed at a musical festival honouring the eighteen-year-old Prince of Wales during his Canadian tour. By 1862, efforts were underway in Montreal to raise money for her musical education, but they met with disappointing results. "The French Canadians had the old-world traditional misgivings of a public career and especially a dislike for anyone belonging to them to go on the stage," she explained many years later. "Consequently all help, as they then honestly thought in my best interests, was withheld."

This was not the case in Albany, New York where she found employment as a church choir leader and organist. The congregation sponsored benefit concerts that helped fund her move to Paris in 1868.

Her tutors were retired operatic tenor Gilbert-Louis Duprez and celebrated teacher Francesco Lamperti. "She has a beautiful voice and a sacred fire," Duprez said of her talent. "She is the wood from which the finest flutes are made."

Just before her first professional singing engagement, an elocution teacher suggested a name change and she chose the old Italian family name "Albani," possibly in salute to her New York state supporters. Her debut in 1869 debut in Messina, Sicily was a triumph. The *Sicilian Courier* described Emma Albani as "a privileged creature, in whom both the lady and the artist stand at the same eminence, and in whom the actress and the singer are in unison."

Accolades at Covent Garden in London followed.

She enjoyed a long association with that prestigious company, which included marrying the manager, Ernest Gye.

The stunning diva performed throughout Great Britain, Europe and the United States before returning to Canada. Her repertoire included forty operas and forty-three different roles, as well as ballads such as "Annie Laurie" and "The Bluebells of Scotland" which were favourites of her friend, Queen Victoria. Kaiser Wilhelm I (Victoria's cousin) favoured her interpretations of Richard Wagner's epic operas so much that he made Albani a royal court singer. Critics praised her voice, and composers delighted in the accuracy of her interpretations.

In 1896, Albani toured Canada from Halifax to Victoria, earning the title "Queen of Song." She made two more Canadian tours before retiring, giving her last public recital in 1911. A Beethoven Medal was just one of her many honours, and in 1925 she was created Dame Commander of the British Empire. Hats and cake recipes were named after Albani, as well as a roadway in Montreal.

To assist her in retirement, the British government provided a small allowance but the Canadian and Quebec governments did nothing to support the widowed singer. Her fans rose to the occasion when the Montreal newspaper, *La Presse*, sponsored a fund-raising campaign and Australian opera star, Nellie Melba, organized similar efforts in England, allowing Albani to live in comfort until her death at eighty-three.

"I have married an Englishman and have made my home in England," she noted in her memoirs, *Forty Years of Song*, "but still remain at heart a French Canadian."

BUCKSKIN AND BROCADE

Brantford, Ontario, 1884 — Poetry readings can be sonorously serious, but when self-proclaimed Mohawk princess Pauline Johnson felt her audience slipping into a trance she simply let out a whoop, called it a war cry, and got back to the business of entertaining. Her mother was British, her father was Mohawk. She drew from both backgrounds and created a persona that served her literary purpose.

Emily Pauline Johnson was a kind of side-show in her own time, trapped in her own legend and torn between two cultures. She often wore two costumes, her beaded buckskins, moccasins and bear-claw native jewelry in the first act and a white brocade evening gown in the second. "There are those who think they pay me a compliment by saying I am just like a white woman," she told a friend. "I am Indian, and my aim, my joy and my pride is to sing the glories of my own people."

Johnson's commitment to her native heritage was grounded in a childhood that would seem the stuff of dreams. Born in 1861, on the reservation of the Six

Nations near Brantford, Ontario, she grew up in an elegant, two-story mansion known as "Chiefswood." Instead of Mother Goose stories, her mother, Emily, raised her on Byron and Keats. By the age of twelve, Johnson said she had read every line Sir Walter Scott and Henry Longfellow ever wrote, and she was well into Shakespeare and Emerson.

Her father's family claimed a Mohawk noble title that dated back to the creation of the League of the Iroquois. Her great-grandfather was baptized Jacob Johnson. He was the godson of Sir William Johnson, the first British superintendent of the northern natives of British North America and consort of Mohawk matriarch Molly Brant. Her grandfather, John "Smoke" Johnson was a story-teller and through him Pauline kept alive her knowledge of the Mohawk language and the legends of her forebears.

Chiefswood was host to many visiting dignitaries, including Prince Arthur, the Duke of Connaught who was initiated into the Mohawk nation at the mansion in 1869. Behind the veil of gentility, Johnson's father, Chief George, waged a battle on the Six Nations reserve against the liquor trade and theft of native timber resources. He was savagely beaten at least twice by non-native interlopers, and died after years of broken health in 1884.

Until this point, Johnson does not seem to have given much thought to a career. At twenty-three she began submitting her work to New York's *Gems of Poetry* and Toronto's *The Week*. At twenty-five, she contributed a poem at the dedication of a statue to Chief Joseph Brant but she was too shy to read it herself. Finally, at thirty, she found her "voice." Wearing her native buckskins, she launched into a rousing reading of *A Cry From an Indian Wife* at a Toronto author's evening for Young Liberals. She was a hit. A second performance was scheduled shortly afterward and Johnson composed *The Song My Paddle Sings* for the event. Performing under her family name, Tekahionwake (meaning "double wampum") she embarked on a tour that culminated in her introduction to English society and the publication of her first book of poems, *The White Wampum*, in 1895.

Poetry, however, was the next best thing to poverty. *Saturday Night* magazine paid the grandiose sum of three dollars to publish *The Song My Paddle Sings*. In her lifetime, she is said to have earned only $500 from her poetry. Johnson was forced to resume a recital career, writing nature sketches, articles and short stories for publications such as *Harper's Weekly*, *The Canadian Magazine* and *The Boy's World* to make ends meet. Although her work resounded with romance, she never married and suffered one ill-fated engagement to a Toronto banking inspector. As fellow-poet Charles Mair once noted: "The defeat of love runs like a grey thread through much of Miss Johnson's verse."

All told, she crossed Canada nineteen times. During this time she teamed up with Walter McRaye, an entertainer fifteen years her junior who performed the *habitant* poems of William Henry Drummond. They barn-stormed from Halifax to Kamloops, speaking in churches, auditoriums and bar rooms. Along the way, Johnson kept writing and, although the results may have suffered a lack of polish, her themes remained Canadian and her personality a constant source of intrigue. In 1906, she returned to London, performing at Steinway Hall. There she met Chief Joe Capilano of the Squamish Mission of North Vancouver who was in England to appeal to King Edward VII to protest restrictions on aboriginal fishing rights.

Three years later, an exhausted Johnson retired from the stage to write prose in Vancouver. She renewed her friendship with Chief Joe and the resulting book, *Legends of Vancouver*, has been lauded by critics as "the first noteworthy rendering of Indian mythic material."

Johnson's health deteriorated and cancer of the breast was diagnosed too late to be operable. The "Mohawk

Princess" died in 1913. "The inspiration of her genius was all Canadian, and all she wrote betrayed her love of the country which has passed from the rule of her fathers into the hands of aliens," declared the *Vancouver Province*.

BEAUTIFUL JOE

Halifax, Nova Scotia, 1893 — Margaret Marshall Saunders was thirty-three when she wrote *Beautiful Joe*, the "autobiography" of an ill-treated but amiable dog, which was published in 1893. The short novel took first prize in an American Humane Society competition, and became an international best-seller of over six million copies in more than forteen languages.

Saunders was born in Milton, Nova Scotia, and enjoyed a classical education. After studying in Scotland and France, she taught school for several years in Halifax, but never warmed to the work. At the suggestion of family and friends she was encouraged to try writing fiction.

In 1889 she published her first novel, a wildly melodramatic romance called *My Spanish Sailor*. To avoid public antipathy to female novelists, she dropped her first name and published androgynously as Marshall Saunders.

Beautiful Joe was inspired by a chance meeting in Meaford, Ontario, where Saunders encountered a local miller, William Moore. He told her the story of a homely puppy he had rescued from a brutal master who had clipped the animal's ears and tail.

From this thread, Saunders wove an unapologetically sentimental story written from the point of view of the abused dog who ultimately finds a home with caring humans. *Beautiful Joe* became the first book by a Canadian to sell more than one million copies.

"I don't believe that a dog could have fallen into a happier home than I did," the mangled mongrel muses, in a conclusion reminiscent of British author Anna Sewell's 1877 best-seller, *Black Beauty*, which surely provided Saunders with inspiration. *Beautiful Joe* became the hit of the 1890s.

Over the next thirty years, Saunders wrote more than twenty-five books, most of them heart-tugging children's stories about domestic animals and birds. She travelled extensively throughout North America lecturing school children and service clubs as an advocate of legislation for wildlife protection and the humane treatment of all animals. Her humanitarian interests were also reflected in *The Girl from Vermont*, which protested the use of child labour in American factories.

In 1914, Saunders moved from Halifax to Toronto, where she lived with her sister, one dog and as many as 200 pet birds. Neighbourhood children regularly brought injured birds and animals to her for treatment. As often as not, they would find the famous author with a pigeon or two riding around on her shoulders.

Her work consistently stressed kindness and she approached human cruelty not as a lack of virtue or of understanding, but as a failure of feeling. Later critics would find much of her work maudlin and didactic, but she wrote with an entertaining grace.

While Marshall Saunders' literary ambition may have been best realized in her ability to wet eyes and wring hearts, other turn of the century authors such as Ernest

Thompson Seton and Charles G. D. Roberts, expanded Canadian literature to include a whole new genre of "animal biography," featuring realistic stories of wild animals.

Subsequent naturalist and conservationist authors include Roderick Haig-Brown and Farley Mowat, whose Canadian nature tales and chronicles for adults and children are as world-renowned today as *Beautiful Joe* was more than a century ago.

THE ORIGINAL ROLLING STONE

Whitehorse, Yukon, 1906 — Robert Service was a bank teller in Whitehorse when he was invited to prepare a reading for a church concert. It was a rowdy Klondike Saturday night when the line: "A bunch of the boys were whooping it up," popped into his head.

After returning to his apartment above the bank office, Service says in his autobiography, *Ploughman of the Moon*, he crept downstairs to the quiet of his teller's cage and commenced work. A sleeping guard awoke and assumed the midnight author was a burglar.

"Fortunately, he was a poor shot or 'The Shooting of Dan McGrew' might never have been written," wrote Service. "With the sensation of a bullet whizzing past my head, and a detonation ringing in my ears, the ballad was achieved." More than fifty years later, Service finally admitted the story was pure hokum.

Service emigrated to Canada from Scotland in 1894 with fifteen dollars in his pocket and visions of becoming a cowboy. He tramped about and took all manner of odd jobs, before he began a career in banking which led him to the Yukon.

His first book of verse, *Songs of a Sourdough*, was an accidental success. Service had intended to print a slim volume of his poems as a souvenir booklet for his friends, and his father forwarded the material to a publisher of hymnals in New York for printing. The book sold itself when pressmen were discovered laughing and reciting Service's verse, including the classic "The Cremation of Sam McGee." The book sold over two million copies and made Service one of the best-known and wealthiest writers in Canada.

In 1908, Service was transferred to Dawson City and he settled in a rustic cabin, which is now a museum. He wrote his first novel here, *The Trail of '98*. When it was finished he decided to deliver it personally to his publisher in New York.

"We expected you to arrive in mukluks and a parka driving a dog team down Fifth Avenue," exclaimed the publisher, who was surprised to find Service rather unassuming in appearance. Far from the rough and tumble, hard-drinking womanizers and scoundrels he immortalized, Service was a teetotaller and a physical fitness buff with a particular passion for potatoes. Nevertheless, the book was deemed bawdy enough to be banned in Boston.

After one of his famous "tramps" to New Orleans and Havana, with a visit to his mother on the Alberta prairies, Service went back to the Klondike and wrote another collection of verse, *Rhymes of a Rolling Stone*. In the autumn of 1912, he took the last steamboat out of Dawson, and never returned.

His life remained action-packed. As a reporter, he covered the Balkan War, and during World War One he served as an ambulance driver and as an intelligence officer for the Canadian Army. His collection of war poetry, *Rhymes of a Red Cross Man*, headed the non-fiction bestseller list in 1917 and 1918.

Dispelling rumours of his death, Service continued to publish both his memoirs and at least eight books of verse, while living comfortably in Monte Carlo and Brittany. A physical fitness book he wrote in 1928 called *Why Not Grow Young? or Living for Longevity*, was reprinted when Service was a spry octogenarian. One of his health tips was to recommend potato eating. He claimed to eat as many as 22,000 tubers a year!

In 1958, Canadian television broadcaster Patrick Watson and journalist Pierre Berton interviewed the eighty-four-year-old, self-proclaimed "rhymer" at his villa overlooking the Mediterranean.

"Say, wouldn't it be a sensation if I croaked in the middle of this interview?" asked Service with a twinkle in his eye. The Bard of the Yukon died a few months later leaving a legacy that is the stuff of myth.

THE LAUGHING ONE

Kitwancool, British Columbia, 1928 — "The woods and sky out West are big. You can't squeeze them down," she once said. Emily Carr was born in 1871, the same year that British Columbia entered Confederation. "Contrary from the start," was the way Carr described herself in her autobiography. She had no use for the tidy conventions of the society of Victoria, B.C.

She was orphaned at sixteen, and two years later her guardian granted her permission to study at the California School of Design in San Francisco. On her return, she established a studio in a cow barn and began giving drawing lessons to children, and saving her money for future studies in Paris and London.

In fact, Carr found the subjects of her greatest art before she left for Europe, when a friend took her to an isolated Vancouver Island mission called Ucluelet in 1898. The tangled, untamed and even menacing forest environment both attracted and repelled her, while the intense artistry of the ancient totem poles moved her deeply, and in the native people themselves she found a kindred spirit. They named her Klee Wyck — the Laughing One.

In Europe, Carr observed the "new art" of the Post Impressionists. She discovered "brilliant, luscious, clean paintings." Her work hung in the Salon d'Automne of 1911 in Paris, and there was clear recognition of her talent. When she returned to Vancouver and exhibited her paintings, by her own account the result was "insult and scorn."

So she turned her back on Vancouver, packed up her paint box and easel and made a harrowing journey up the coast to the Queen Charlotte Islands and remote native villages on the Skeena and Naas Rivers, where she painted the vanishing villages and totem poles.

Unable to live from her art, she became disillusioned and built a small apartment house in Victoria, spending fifteen years as a landlady, and augmenting her income by breeding dogs, hooking rugs and making pottery.

In 1927, she was invited to include her work in an exhibition of West Coast art at the National Art Gallery in Ottawa. Carr admitted at the time that she did not even know that Canada had a National Gallery!

It was a turning point. Her work was enthusiastically received, and she was inspired by the artists of the Group of Seven, whose aspirations matched her own. "Something has spoken to the very soul of me," she wrote in her journal, finding in their canvases "a naked soul, pure and unashamed."

A burst of energy followed in 1928. Carr abandoned her tenants and headed back to the Queen Charlotte Islands to Kitwancool, a remote village noted for its impressive totem poles. She captured the totems with bold reverence, in her own brooding and solemn vision.

In later years, Carr turned her brush to the large rhythms of the coastal rain forests, beaches and skies. Living in a caravan with a menagerie of pets, she painted the grand primeval brooding of the forest, translating the spiritual essence of the light in scenes of constant visual movement.

"At last, I knew that I must see through the eye of the totem — the mythic eye of the forest," she wrote. Before she died in 1945, Emily Carr was in the first rank of Canadian painters.

IS IT A BIRD? IS IT A PLANE? NO! IT'S A CANUCK!

Cleveland, Ohio, 1934 — "Truth, justice and the American way," a phenomenon administered by a muscle man wearing a cape and tights, but Superman, the king of the comic super-heroes, was the creation of a Canadian.

Joe Shuster came up with the idea of a "strange visitor from another planet with powers and abilities far beyond those of mortal men" with his buddy, Jerry Siegal, when the pair were only seventeen years old. Shuster was living in Cleveland, Ohio at the time, but had grown up in Toronto along with most of his family including cousin Frank, whose own fame would come as half of Canada's "Wayne and Shuster" comedy team. He started drawing as a child, and he drew on anything and everything that was free, including discarded butcher paper and the back-side of abandoned wallpaper rolls.

According to novelist Mordecai Richler, Superman can be seen as a perfect expression of the Canadian psyche. Shuster's mighty Man of Steel hides his extraordinary strength, speed, and superhuman powers under the bland, self-effacing guise of the weak and clumsy Clark Kent, mild-mannered reporter.

Superman is a hero who does not take any credit for his own heroism. He is a glamorous figure who could get the best table in any restaurant, but is content to live his daily life in horned-rimmed glasses and brown suits and carry his lunch to work. With his modest alter-ego Clark Kent, who, however meek, does seem to get scoop after scoop, Superman is the archetypal Canadian personality who became a "universal hero," famed throughout the world as the champion of everything virtuous.

Shuster modeled *The Daily Planet*, where Clark Kent was gainfully employed, after Toronto's *Daily Star*. The cityscape of Metropolis, the fictional city that Superman vowed to clean up, was patterned after Toronto in the 1930s. Indeed, when he was not moving faster than a speeding bullet and leaping over tall buildings in a single bound, Superman reverted to being a shy, bespectacled guy, not unlike Joe Shuster himself.

Superman leaped from comic books to radio in the 1940s, and onto the television screen by the 1950s. By the late 1970s he was a movie star. Even *Superman the Movie* had many Canadian connections. The small town sequences were all shot in High River, Alberta. Actor Glen Ford, who hailed from Quebec, played Superman's adoptive father and Regina-born Margot Kidder played the intrepid Lois Lane.

Unfortunately, Shuster saw few of the rewards reaped by the "Metropolis Marvel's" success. He and Siegel invented their x-ray visioned character in 1934, but it took four years for D.C. Comics to hire the persistent pair and place Superman on the cover of *Action Comics* Number One in 1938. Four issues later, it was a runaway success, but Shuster and Siegel had already sold the rights to their creation to the publisher for $130 U.S.

When the pair sued to regain control in 1947, they

lost and were fired as *Superman*'s artist and writer. By 1975, Shuster was legally blind, living in a rundown New York City apartment. Growing knowledge of his plight prompted Warner Communications, which had bought the rights to *Superman* for their 1978 blockbuster movie, to award the creators a yearly stipend of $20,000 each. As Brad Roberts, lead singer for the Winnipeg-based, internationally successful rock band "Crash Test Dummies" put it in his 1991 ballad *Superman Song*: "Superman never made any money..." but Joe Shuster's creation was never about anything so crass as capital gain.

Superman is about the inevitable triumph of good over evil and the ability to change clothes in telephone booths. The character stands at the top of the twentieth century cultural pantheon, as globally recognizable as Mickey Mouse, Charlie Chaplin and Elvis. "There aren't many people who can honestly say they'll be leaving behind something as important as Superman," Joe Shuster told the *Toronto Star* on the newspaper's 100th anniversary. Two months later, on June 30, 1992, Joe Shuster died at seventy-eight.

PART 6

ADVENTURE AND DISCOVERY

THE PIRATE ADMIRAL

Harbour Grace, Newfoundland, 1610 — Maritime outlaw Peter Easton, a short, dark man with a glib tongue and a cruel streak, offset by his good cheer and generosity, remains a folk hero in Newfoundland. The town of Happy Adventure is named for his flagship, and many of his adopted pirates took the Easton name in his honour.

While Samuel de Champlain was struggling to found his colony at Quebec, commerce was booming in St. John's. The Basques, Portuguese, French and English gathered at the harbour to trade and refit their ships.

Easton's first visit to Newfoundland was during the reign of Queen Elizabeth I. He came with her blessing as a privateer. When James I took the throne, he eliminated the legal plundering of foreign ships by privateers, which led to a massive transition to outright piracy.

Easton made the transition quite successfully. By 1610 he commanded forty ships and he was the recognized leader of a loose federation of pirates engaged in looting ships in the English Channel.

Merchants petitioned the government for relief from Easton's depredations, and Sir Henry Mainwarring prepared a squadron of ships to pursue Easton. However, Easton avoided any engagement by embarking for Newfoundland.

He arrived with ten armed ships and built a fort at Harbour Grace, where he proceeded to recruit — or press — fishermen into his service.

Although he used Harbour Grace primarily as a base, he found time to raid Basque and French ships for their arms, commandeered cargoes of salt fish and "liberated" at least one shipload of French wine.

In Conception Bay he took two ships and thirty ships were pillaged in St. John's. The colony at Cupids was spared after rendering two pigs to the buccaneer. Easton even stored and protected the colonists' valuable fishing supplies and tons of salt during the winter. Often accompanied by trumpeters and minstrels, his loyal followers dubbed him the "Pirate Admiral" and he was perceived as a defender of common folk.

By 1612, Easton had amassed a considerable navy. He is said to have taken 500 fishermen into his employ. The *Happy Adventure* alone required a crew of 150.

Easton's greatest coup during this period was a raid conducted in Puerto Rico. Although the Spanish colony at Moro Castle had withstood an attack by Sir Francis Drake, Easton and his Newfoundland pirates made off with stockpiles of gold and returned with a Spanish ship filled with treasure.

Basques had captured his fort in his absence, and the triumphant return ended in a battle on land and sea. Forty-seven men died regaining Easton's fort and they are buried at nearby Bear's Cove, in a place still known as "the Pirates' Graveyard."

Although he was an outlaw in England, Easton applied to King James for a pardon, and apparently paid well for it. In fact, he received two pardons.

En route to his retirement, Easton paused to intercept the Spanish plate fleet which was transporting the annual loot of the empire from Central America.

When he finally settled down in a palace on the French Riviera, Easton was one of the richest men in the world. He became a marquis, and lived in the lap of luxury.

Easton never returned to Newfoundland, but his fishermen pirates did and the Easton name remains popular in that part of Newfoundland where pirates once reigned.

MANDARIN OF THE MISSISSIPPI

Lake Michigan, 1634 — Twenty-year-old Jean Nicollet was fresh from his studies in Paris when he arrived in Quebec in 1618 with a handful of fellow citizens and four priests. He had been hired to live among the native people, and to encourage them to collect furs to trade with the French.

In the early years of the seventeenth century, the beaver-pelt trade created a heated rivalry among the French, English and Dutch. While the English and Dutch tried to attract native people to their trading posts, the French lived among them, learning their languages and customs, and converting them to Christianity.

Samuel de Champlain, who had established the first upriver trading post on the St. Lawrence in 1608, sent Nicollet to Allumette Island, a strategic outpost on the Ottawa River. His assignment was to create friendly relations with the Algonkians, an allegiance the French needed to counteract the Dutch influence with the Iroquois to the south.

For Nicollet it meant entering a strange and harsh

new life. He accompanied the Algonkians on canoeing, hunting and trapping expeditions; acquiring their language and adapting to their customs in the process. He carted heavy pelts through deep snow, ate raw game and learned to portage in bare feet. Although the solitude was not easy for the young Parisian, Nicollet's endurance, resourcefulness, and patience earned him the respect of the Algonkians. He was even able to help them negotiate peace with the Iroquois.

Next he was sent northwest to Lake Nippissing where he founded a trading post. He spent nine years doing business with various tribes and journeying into the Great Lakes region where he collected precious geographical information. In the spring, he sent pelts to Quebec.

Since Jacques Cartier's first expedition in 1534, explorers had dreamed of finding a passage to China that would give Europeans easy access to its spices, silks and precious metals. One hundred years later, Champlain challenged Nicollet with a dual mission. The Winnebagoes, who lived on the western shore of Lake Michigan, had strained relations with the Algonkians and threatened to ally themselves with the Dutch. Along with his diplomatic duties, Nicollet was commissioned to verify reports of "the great water" called "Mississippi," which he presumed led to China. The Winnebagoes were known as the "people of the sea," and rumour had it that they "had neither hair nor beards" and had come from the Orient. Nicollet set off to cross Lakes Ontario, Erie and Huron by canoe in search of the route to untold riches.

When the eager explorer reached the Winnebagoes, the scene may have resembled something out of a slapstick comedy. Nicollet was so convinced he had reached the gateway to China that he donned a dress of Chinese damask embroidered with coloured birds and flowers. Dressed for success and brandishing two pistols, he disembarked.

The Winnebagoes had never seen a European, let

alone one who was dressed to meet Chinese mandarins. However, once they became accustomed to the charming ambassador, Nicollet convinced them to join in peaceful trade. Unfortunately, Nicollet's "great water" turned out to be Lake Michigan, but he had ventured further west than any other European. Others would follow to chart the heart of the continent.

In 1642, Nicollet accidentally drowned in the icy waters of the St. Lawrence. Ironically, the adventurer who had spent most of his life travelling the lakes, rivers and streams of the New World had never learned to swim.

THE SCENT OF A MAMMAL

New France, 1685 — New France represented a cornucopia of new plant and animal life to its explorers. Among these never-before-seen oddities, the skunk was no uncertain surprise to eager settlers who had never experienced its "nature."

Michel Sarrazin, the colony's first natural scientist, abandoned an attempt to analyze the creature's anatomy because "it had a frightful smell, capable of making a whole canton [district] desert."

The twenty-six-year-old French surgeon came to New France in 1685 and became Surgeon-Major of the troops at Ville-Marie and Quebec City. He also served the civilian population and treated several well-known citizens for wounds they received during duels.

Sarrazin's hobby was scientific endeavour and he devoted himself to investigating the indigenous flora and fauna, which presented many uncharted species. Initially, he would risk Iroquois ambush while roaming the woods, fields and bogs, gathering specimens and assembling countless notes and sketches which he forwarded to scientists in France. "I could more easily traverse the whole of Europe, with less danger, than I could cover 100 leagues in Canada," he wrote.

In 1699 the Royal Academy of Sciences in Paris honoured Sarrazin by naming him as a corresponding member. Attempts were made to ship potted bushes and plants to France on the King's ship. Sailors were instructed to maintain them on the deck, and in the absence of rain they were to utilize precious reserves from the ship's meagre water supply. This proved futile, since the plants were often drenched by waves of salt water and Intendant Bochart de Champigny received correspondence indicating that the samples arrived "dry, or more exactly dead." Seeds fared better, and samples of Canadian flora were soon growing in the King's royal garden.

Sarrazin's "hobby" did not interfere with his duties as a doctor and he was considered quite competent. Although surgical techniques were far from advanced and anesthetics quite primitive, in 1700 Sarrazin performed a breast cancer operation on a nun. It may have been the first of its kind in New France and his biographer, Arthur Vallée, cites this as an example of Sarrazin's "professional conscious, surgical ability and religious and moral valour."

Epidemics of flu and yellow fever were a constant problem. In his quest for cures and remedies, Sarrazin gained the trust of the native people and sought their suggestions. Following a smallpox epidemic in 1702 that killed 2,000 people, Sarrazin employed his botanical skills to discover a smallpox treatment through the common pitcher plant, whose scientific name became *Sarracenia purpurea*.

Industry in the colony also benefitted from Sarrazin's love of nature. His investigation into the properties of the sugar maple laid the foundation for the harvest of maple syrup, which reduced the need for expensive, imported sugar. By 1704, Sarrazin had submitted more than 200 specimens to the Royal Academy, including exhaustive anatomical studies of the beaver, porcupine and muskrat.

As a member of the Superior Council, his knowledge of plant life was applied to agriculture and he was charged with the responsibility of examining the milling and cooking of wheat. Although Turkish wheat was initially considered, Sarrazin obtained hardier wheat specimens from Sweden which yielded better results.

At fifty-three, Sarrazin married a woman thirty-three years his junior. The marriage certificate shows Sarrazin's age as only forty, which may have been a touch of coquettish gallantry on his part. Although he owned many properties, medicine was not particularly lucrative due to the lack of hard currency in New France. When he died at seventy-five from typhus brought over on one of the ships, Michel Sarrazin was a pauper.

"He exercised his art with a rare and unselfish charity, serving all who sought his help with kindness and grace which he dispensed equally and with great success," reported the Sisters of L'Hôtel Dieu hospital.

The skunk may have eluded Sarrazin, but his contribution to the health of New France and the understanding of its unique natural world set a precedent of excellence for others to follow.

THE ORIGINAL BIG MAC

Dundela, Ontario, 1811 — The world famous McIntosh apple may have genetic roots to the first apple tree ever planted in Canada, but when it was discovered it was growing wild. Ultimately, it proved to be truly one of a kind.

In 1633, an apple tree called the "Fameuse" was brought to New France from Normandy. It was an instant success and apples became a prized fruit on pioneer farms, since they could be stored in root cellars, dried or pressed into cider.

In 1811, John McIntosh was clearing land to build his farmhouse in Dundas County, in eastern Ontario. In the undergrowth, he discovered some seedling apple trees, which he transplanted.

One tree in particular produced exceptionally firm, red apples with sweet, juicy flesh. While other apple trees fell prey to the cold weather and disease, this particular tree was the hardiest producer in the neighbourhood.

McIntosh's son, Allan, attempted to grow seedlings from the tree in the 1820s, however, none of the seedlings bore the same crisp fruit as the old tree. The original tree was self-sterile and pollen from other apple trees that fertilized the blossoms produced a good tree, but not quite the original.

The young McIntosh knew there had to be a solution. As a Methodist minister, he travelled the countryside always carrying a supply of the unique apples, which were affectionately known as "Granny's Treats." Farmers throughout the countryside were impressed, but no one could solve the mystery of reproducing the tree.

Just as his father discovered the tree by chance, Allan McIntosh discovered the solution to his tree reproduction dilemma through a curious coincidence of fate.

In 1835, an American farm labourer arrived one spring day looking for work, and over a glass of "Granny" cider he learned about the McIntosh conundrum. The man suggested that the solution lay in grafting a small branch from the original tree to another variety of apple rootstock.

The hired man spent the summer instructing McIntosh in the art of grafting, budding and pruning. Then he left, never to be heard from again. Soon farmers were able to buy grafted seedlings, and the fame of the "McIntosh Red" spread.

By 1862, apple trees had been planted across the nation. Along with the McIntosh, the Baldwin, Russet, Greening and Snow apple trees flourished, while other varieties such as the Winter Codlin and Seek-No-Further all but disappeared.

At the turn of the century, half of the orchards in Ontario were producing McIntosh apples, and McIntosh Reds were finding popularity in the United States. Disaster struck in 1895 when a fire broke out and the original tree was scorched. Allan McIntosh himself propped barn doors around it to protect it from the blaze and he spent months nursing it back to health. The tree had become something of a celebrity in its own right.

The original McIntosh apple tree outlived Allan McIntosh by eleven years. It produced fruit until 1908 and finally toppled in 1910, but its progeny continue to thrive throughout Canada and the world.

LET THERE BE LIGHT

Charlottetown, Prince Edward Island, 1846 — Long before the light bulb, kerosene changed the nocturnal habits of nations. It was the discovery of a failed horse trader and self-taught geologist named Abraham Gesner. More than kerosene, his methods and processes of distilling oil from hydrocarbons led to the establishment of the entire petrochemical industry. In 1933, Imperial Oil erected a monument honouring him as the "American inventor" of kerosene, but Abraham Gesner was a true Canadian genius.

He was a farmer's son, born in 1797 and raised near Cornwallis, Nova Scotia. In his youth, he collected rocks and dabbled in chemistry. When several of his "experiments" resulted in explosions in the homestead, a makeshift laboratory was established in a shed. Young Gesner impressed some local farmers with his homemade matches, while others were convinced his destiny was to blow himself to smithereens.

Jobs were scarce, so Gesner turned to horse trading.

He planned to ship horses to the West Indies for profit, a concept that was as risky as it was inhumane. His first venture barely broke even, nevertheless he returned with mineral samples, including a curious black "pitch" from Trinidad which proved to be ashphaltum. In his early experiments with the sticky substance, Gesner discovered that it burned with a hot, steady flame. If the problems of smoke and smell could be eliminated, it might even make an illuminant.

But commerce called. Gesner was anxious to earn enough money to marry a doctor's daughter, Harriet Webster. His subsequent horse-trading ventures floundered, quite literally, and instead of being penniless, he found himself in debt.

Although he managed to marry Harriet, Gesner's father-in-law sent him to medical school in England to avoid disgrace at the hands of his creditors.

Returning to Nova Scotia in 1827, he chose Parrsboro as the location for his practice, more for its interesting terrain than for its medical prospects. During this time, he travelled the countryside on horseback in the company of Micmac Indians, playing the flute while they helped him gather geological specimens.

His treatises on the geology and mineralogy of Nova Scotia established his reputation and from 1838 to 1842 he served New Brunswick as its first geologist. His enthusiastic reports led several speculators to rush into ventures that went bankrupt and the government refused to pay Gesner for his final year.

This time Gesner confronted debt with the novel idea of opening a paid-admission museum. In St. John, he assembled 2,173 artifacts from his private collection, including numerous fossils and oddities such as the air bladder of a sturgeon. When it failed, his creditors accepted the collection in place of payment and it formed part of the foundation of the New Brunswick Museum.

Gesner returned to medical practise in Cornwallis, devoting his spare time to refining hydrocarbons in the same laboratory shed he had enjoyed as a child. At an 1846 lecture in Charlottetown, Prince Edward Island, he introduced a substance he called "keroselain" after a Greek word meaning "wax oil." It was a clear, white oil that he distilled from the treated vapours of heated coal.

Candles, whale oil and other illuminants of the day produced dingy light and greasy, odorous smoke. "Burning fluid" composed of turpentine and alcohol produced a bright light, often accompanied by explosions. Gesner's oil could be handled easily and burned with a brilliant yellow light that produced almost no smoke. He refined his process further when he identified a previously unknown mineral, albertite, a bitumen found in Albert County, New Brunswick. Gesner bought a large tract of land containing the mineral, only to have that venture land him in court when another man claimed the coal rights. A jury was bamboozled into believing that albertite and coal were one and the same. Gesner's loss turned into a multi-million dollar profit for his adversary.

Embittered and impoverished, Gesner left Canada. He had secured patents in the United States and wealthy developers in Long Island, New York, set up a factory under his guidance in 1854. "Kerosene" became the most successful lamp oil ever produced, but Gesner was never a partner in the profits. His patent was challenged and, once again, Gesner lost.

He died in 1864, just as he was about to become the first chemistry professor at Dalhousie University.

SERVING IN A HOUSE DIVIDED

Washington, D.C., 1865 — More than 50,000 Canadians served in the American Civil War. One of them, Anderson Ruffin Abbott, distinguished himself by becoming one of only eight black surgeons to administer to the wounds of Union soldiers. He became a friend of the family of Abraham Lincoln, and he appears to have been the first black man to attend a White House levee. Following Lincoln's assassination in 1865, his wife, Mary Todd, presented Abbott with the black-and-white, Shepherd Plaid shawl that the sixteenth President had worn on the day of his first inauguration.

Abbott's father, Wilson, was born of free parents in Richmond, Virginia. As a young man, Wilson and his wife, Ellen, operated a general store in Mobile, Alabama. When the city council of Mobile passed a law requiring free blacks to wear a badge indicating that they had posted a bond signed by two white men guaranteeing their good behaviour, Wilson Abbott refused to comply. An anonymous threat followed, and the couple decided to relocate quickly.

Shortly afterward, their store was burned to the ground.

They came to Toronto in 1835. Two years later Anderson Ruffin was born. The couple was active in church and anti-slavery organizations, and Ellen Toyer Abbott founded the Queen's Benevolent Society, which aided black refugees.

When his tobacco shop failed, Wilson Abbott began to buy property and rent houses. He had learned to read and write from his wife, and he possessed a natural ability in mathematics. Over the next forty years, he acquired more than seventy-five properties in Toronto and throughout southwestern Ontario. The value of his holdings is impossible to estimate, however, among the tracts that he once owned in Toronto are the sites of the City Hall and the Eaton Centre.

The Abbotts raised three children, all of whom received the best possible education. Anderson Ruffin attended the prestigious Buxton School in Chatham, Ontario, the Toronto Academy and Oberlin College in Ohio before enrolling in the Toronto School of Medicine. In 1861, he became the first Canadian-born black to be licensed in the practice of medicine.

Dr. Abbott was determined to join the Union Army. When blacks were finally permitted to participate in 1863, he was appointed as a surgeon at Freedman's Hospital in Washington. Soon afterward he became Surgeon-in-Charge of the 2,000 bed military hospital at Camp Baker.

Even Abbott's surviving family are uncertain about his connection to Lincoln. He was known to have been the personal physician to Mary Todd Lincoln's dressmaker. Whatever circumstances forged the friendship, it was powerful enough for Mrs. Lincoln to feel that her husband's shawl should be passed to Abbott as a token of appreciation to all Canadians who had joined the Civil War effort.

Many blacks who had sought refuge in Canada prior to the Emancipation Proclamation moved back to the

United States, but Abbott returned to his Canadian roots.

He married and settled in Chatham where he practised medicine and became the first black coroner in Canada. He was constantly investigating new medical techniques and promoted high standards among his colleagues. As president of the Wilberforce Educational Institute, Abbott lobbied for equal education for all races.

In 1894, he moved to Chicago, where he served as Medical Superintendent of the Provident Hospital which had been founded by the black community as both a hospital and a nurses' training school.

When he retired in Toronto, Abbott continued to lecture in medicine and wrote articles protesting discrimination wherever he found it.

Toward the end of his life, Abbott reflected on his participation in the Civil War. "I am a Canadian, first and last and all the time, but that did not deter me from sympathizing with a nation struggling to wipe out an inequity," he wrote. "It was not a war for conquest or territorial aggrandizement, nor for racial, social or political supremacy. It was not a war for white men or black men, red men or yellow men. It was a war for humanity, a conflict between beautiful right and ugly wrong, between civilization and barbarism, between freedom and slavery. Canadians have a right to claim a full share in the honour and glory of that achievement."

A MAN FOR ALL TIME ZONES

Toronto, 1879 — When it is 6:00 p.m. in Prince George, British Columbia, it is 10:30 p.m. in Grand Falls, Newfoundland. Why? The answer is Standard Time, the globally recognized system of telling time which was invented by a Scottish-born Canadian, Sir Sandford Fleming.

Fleming was eighteen when he arrived in Canada prepared to take up a career as a draughtsman and surveyor. After completing the survey of several small Ontario towns, he set about mapping the city of Toronto, producing the first usable chart of Toronto's harbour by taking soundings both from a boat and through holes drilled in the winter ice.

Fleming's interest in developing a universal system of time developed during his work as the Chief Engineer of the Inter-Continental Railroad and the Canadian Pacific Railroad.

In Canada and other countries 12:00 noon was designated as the time when the sun was directly overhead. As a result, if it was noon in Kingston, it was twelve minutes after noon in Montreal and thirteen minutes before noon in Toronto. Local people were perfectly content with local time. After all, they did not have programmable VCRs to concern themselves with. They worked according to the cycle of the season and the placement of the sun.

The variations became more significant when railroads allowed longer distances of travel over shorter time periods. The results were confusing. For example, a journey by train from Halifax to Windsor involved having to re-set your watch ten times!

Fleming had a talent for spotting a simple solution to an inconvenient problem. After missing several trains himself and recognizing the headache transcontinental travel would pose, he began examining the history of time. He discovered that most ancient civilizations had computed day and night in twelve-hour cycles. He combined this into a twenty-four-hour clock and proceeded to divide the globe into twenty-four equal zones.

When he first presented the concept of Standard Time to the Canadian Institute for the Advancement of Scientific Knowledge at Toronto in 1879, Fleming was variously denounced as an Utopian and a promoter of notions which were "contrary to the will of God." Persistance and persuasion finally won governments and the scientific community to the practicality of his idea.

Canada adopted Standard Time in 1883, along with all North American railway companies. The following year twenty-five nations adopted the proposition at a conference in Washington, D.C. Greenwich, England was designated as the Prime Meridian (line of longitude) as the base for calculation, since it had served as the standard for two-thirds of the world's shipping industry for many years.

By the late nineteenth century, inhabitants of all but the remotest corners of the world had adopted Standard Time. Coordinated Universal Time, based on atomic clocks established in Paris in 1972, has been the foundation of Standard Time since 1985.

Sandford Fleming was a man of many accomplishments. He designed Canada's first postage stamp, the Threepenny Beaver in 1851. He also lithographed the first accurate large-scale surveyor's maps of Canada and promoted a submarine telegraph cable from Vancouver to Australia. In 1897, Fleming was knighted, but he always contended that his greatest honour was to serve as Chancellor of Queen's University for thirty-five years. Somewhere between his writing of scientific papers and his abiding interest in a good game of chess, Sir Sandford Fleming also wrote an interdenominational prayer book, hymnal and psalter.

"Nothing can be recalled what is past, no not even a second a go," the "Father of Standard Time" once wrote in his diary. "Every action is as it were recorded on the minute of time for ever and ever! I do not regret the time I have spent."

ALBERTOSAURUS, I PRESUME

Alberta Badlands, 1884 — Even with the success of Hollywood blockbuster movies like *Jurassic Park*, few people are aware that at least twenty-five species of dinosaurs mysteriously ended their reign over large areas of Saskatchewan, Alberta and British Columbia at the epilogue of the Mesozoic age. The Plains Indians called them the "grandfathers of the buffalo," and one of those egg-layers, which became extinct over sixty-five million years ago, bears the name of the province in which its mortal remains were discovered.

It is called Albertosaurus and it was a close cousin to the most fearsome of all dinosaurs, the carnivorous Tyrannosaurus. Scientists estimate that Albertosaurus may have grown up to nine metres long and weighed as much as two tonnes.

Its fossilized remains were discovered in 1884 by a young Canadian geologist and explorer named Joseph Burr Tyrrell. At twenty-five, he worked for the Canadian Geological Survey, whose job it was to map the vast territories of Canada in the last century.

Tyrrell and his assistant were paddling their canoe between the steep banks of the Red Deer River, south of Drumheller in southern Alberta. In the layers of ancient rock, the geologist found seams of coal, outcroppings of one of the largest deposits in North America.

On June 9th, Tyrrell set off on his usual routine of examining the river banks when a peculiar brown substance sticking out from the valley wall caught his attention. He scaled the steep slope and, with mounting excitement, he began to clear away the dirt. Using his bare hands and his geologist's hammer, he gradually uncovered the fossilized skeleton of a dinosaur.

Dinosaur remains had been unearthed in western Canada before, but as Tyrrell explored the valley he recognized that nothing like this dinosaur graveyard had ever been found.

One memorable day, after a month of surveying and collecting fossils, Tyrrell looked the ancient past directly in the face. Sixty-nine years later, at the age of ninety-five, he recounted the instant of his most dramatic discovery. "I was climbing up a steep face about 400 feet [120 metres] high. I stuck my head around a point and there was this skull leering at me, sticking right out of the ground. It gave me a fright."

Tyrrell had found the first skull of Albertosaurus.

The "find" was to become the site of the world's richest palaeontological discovery. The skeletal remains of more than 475 dinosaurs have been recovered from the barren valley walls of the Red Deer River.

Although the word dinosaur stems from the Greek *dino saurus* meaning "terrible lizard," recent advances in technology have led scientists to speculate that, unlike reptiles, the dinosaurs may have been warm-blooded creatures more closely linked to animals and birds than lizards and crocodiles.

Dinosaur "nests," fossilized eggs and the remains of

baby dinosaurs have furthered our understanding of the "community" of dinosaurs, and scientific examinations of ancient layers of rock may one day lead to a final understanding of why the dinosaurs disappeared.

Today, the Royal Tyrrell Museum of Palaeontology in Dinosaur Provincial Park in Drumheller, Alberta, pursues the work Joseph Burr Tyrrell started when he took Albertosaurus' skull out of the badlands on the back of a buckboard wagon and gave it to the world.

THE SPIRIT OF TILIKUM

Nootka, British Columbia, 1901 — A Canadian adventurer taught the Governor of Samoa to play poker and ended up playing a major role in saving the buffalo from extinction in western Canada but does anyone remember his name?

Norman Luxton was a man of many careers, travels and travails. He was born in Winnipeg in 1876 and his father, William, was one of the founders of the *Winnipeg Free Press.*

Young Luxton tried his hand at the newspaper business in Calgary and Vancouver, and prospected for gold in the Kootenay area of British Columbia in the early 1900s.

Adventure beckoned when he encountered a kindred spirit in a Danish mariner, Captain F. C. Voss. The pair made plans for a South Seas expedition. Luxton purchased a nine-metre, red-cedar dugout canoe from a Nuu-Cha-Nulth craftsman. Its ungainly renovations included a small cabin, three masts, four sails and an ancient Spanish cannon.

The distinctive craft was christened *Tilikum* — meaning friend. The adventurers departed Nootka, British Columbia on July 6th, 1901, with rudimentary navigational technology, including a sextant with a cracked mirror and a chart showing their approximate destination. On a good day, they could cover 240 kilometres.

By the time Luxton and Voss reached the South Seas, their friendship was strained and they spent most of their time sitting at opposite ends of the vessel clutching their guns, but they were determined to continue.

Finances ran thin when they reached Samoa, so Luxton set himself up as a professor of card games, specializing in poker — which became the particular affection of the Governor.

All told, Luxton and Voss stopped at forty-two South Seas ports to a variety of receptions. One king was so taken with Luxton that he offered him a choice of daughters for marriage and a coconut grove of his own. On another island, a confrontation with hostile residents who were presumed to be "cannibals" called the ancient cannon to their defense.

Luxton abandoned the expedition to recover from injuries suffered in a shipwreck off Australia, but Voss successfully guided the *Tilikum* to England, arriving in September 1904.

Luxton returned to Canada and settled in Banff, Alberta, where he began a publishing business, a trading post and a year-round hotel. He committed himself to the community, leading his biographers to nickname him "the oracle of Banff." During a card game, he helped conceive the Winter Carnival and in the summer Luxton conducted the annual Indian Days Festival in conjunction with the Stoney.

When an influenza epidemic struck near a trading post Luxton operated in northerly Morely, he supplied much-needed food and medical supplies to the isolated native population withoutcompensation. The business failed, but Luxton was named an Honourary Chief of both the Blackfoot and the Stoney tribes.

In 1909, Luxton suggested that the Canadian government purchase a herd of Montana buffalo to replenish the prairie herds which had been hunted almost to the point of extinction. These animals provided the foundation stock for the herds at Wainwright National Park.

Norman Luxton's legacy of adventure and open-hearted vision of the true meaning of "tilikum," continues to thrive. Today, the original dugout *Tilikum* is permanently berthed in Victoria, B.C., and every year thousands of visitors enjoy the spirit of place and the spirit of this unique Canadian adventurer at the Luxton Museum, which is housed in a log building beside the Bow River at Banff.

MASTICATION AS THE MOTHER OF INVENTION

Ottawa, 1907 — There once was a Canadian scientist who chewed his way to a kind of fame and fortune. Through an elaborate process of mastication and elimination, Charles Saunders discovered the wheat strain that made Canada the breadbasket of the world. Still obscure after all these years, Saunders was a reluctant agricultural researcher.

His father, William, a druggist from London, Ontario maintained a passion for horticulture and from an early age all five of the Saunders children were taught the Latin names of plants. Charles was a frail child. Although he dreamed of studying music and enjoyed playing the flute, his father preferred him to study chemistry, so he attended the University of Toronto. "I am a docile person," he once noted. "I am always going where I am pushed."

After completing his studies at Johns Hopkins University and teaching chemistry in Kentucky, Saunders escaped the influence of his father briefly, studying singing and teaching music at a ladies' college.

But Saunders Sr. was bent on having his son carry on

the work he had started in developing a strain of wheat that would ripen early enough to survive fall frosts in the west. In 1885, William Saunders became the director of the Dominion Experimental Farms where he conducted research.

At every vacation, Charles and his brother, Percy, were called upon to apply their knowledge of chemistry to developing new strains. In 1902, Charles Saunders was appointed as Dominion Cerealist — by his father.

It was a tedious task to check each sample, but Saunders was a meticulous researcher. Selection was rigorous. Strains had to be grown separately and individual seed heads demonstrating the greatest strengths were tested.

Wheat could not be milled practically in small lots, which meant it could take years of careful harvest before enough of an experimental strain could be gathered to test its flour and bread-making qualities.

Ultimately, mastication became the mother of invention, when Saunders discovered that, by simply chewing a sample of kernels, he could determine its level of gluten and the sort of bread it would make. He diligently chewed his way through more than 100 varieties before discovering "Markham," a cross between Canadian Red Fife wheat and an Indian variety called Hard Red Calcutta. Feeling that the name was not noble enough, Saunders dubbed it "Marquis" and sent a sackful to the Experimental Farm at Indian Head, Saskatchewan for testing in 1907.

Panic set in when the boss, Angus Mackay, could not find the precious seed sample. An urgent call went out, and the wheat was returned by one of the men who had inadvertently taken it home to feed his chickens.

Marquis wheat proved to be everything Saunders had hoped for. It yielded more bushels than its predecessors and, most importantly, it ripened for harvest one week earlier than Red Fife. When it was released for commercial production in 1909, Marquis became the wheat that won the west. Northern areas were settled, and wheat returns amounted to millions of dollars benefitting manufacturers, merchants and railroads, as well as farmers. By 1920, ninety percent of the wheat grown in western Canada was Marquis.

Saunders suffered a physical breakdown in 1922. He went to Paris where he studied French literature, producing a book of verse and essays which Quebec critics extolled as "courageous." Music remained the passion of his life, although his scientific endeavours earned him a knighthood in 1934.

When Sir Charles Saunders died in 1937, the *Daily Express* of London wrote "he contributed more to the wealth of his country than any other man."

FATHER GOOSE

Kingsville, Ontario, 1908 — Jack Miner was a freckle-faced thirteen-year-old when he became a skunk hunter, earning fifty cents a pelt. This odiferous pursuit helped support his family, including eleven siblings, who moved across Lake Erie from Ohio to seven acres of brush near Kingsville, Ontario in 1878. Young Miner became a "market" hunter. For a bounty fee, barefoot Jack and his brother, Charlie, could kill as many as a dozen rattlesnakes in a day. A bag of twenty ruffed grouse was merely average for the precocious hunter.

"Market hunting is not sport. It is murder in the first degree," Miner later wrote in his autobiography *Wild Goose Jack*. Yet the man who was to receive the Order of the British Empire for his achievements in conservation, spent fully half his life in the killing fields before devoting himself to the preservation issues that led him to establish one of the first bird sanctuaries in North America.

Most of Miner's early life was spent studying nature. His formal education totalled only three months. When he was not working in the family's tile and brick works, he was sought after as a guide for hunting parties. Without a trace of bravado, Miner noted that he and his brother, Ted, "could kill a deer about any time we wanted one."

In 1898, on a moose hunting trip in Northern Ontario, Ted Miner was killed by a careless shot from another hunter. In his grief, Jack was persuaded to go to church, where he volunteered to teach a rowdy boys, Sunday school class. He enthused the boys with his woodsman's adventures and prompted them to read biblical passages relating to nature. In return, the boys taught Miner to read.

Although he continued to take pleasure in hunting, Miner grew steadily more interested in befriending his prey. "Any man who isn't big enough to change his mind has nothing to change," he liked to say. Miner changed his mind about hunting when he perceived that a gaggle of Canada geese could clearly identify him as "the enemy" despite his persuasive imitation of their "khonk, khonk" clarion call.

From that day forward, he embarked on a mission to become a friend of migrating fowl. In 1904, he dug ponds on his farm, planted trees and installed four pinioned Canada geese as decoys. Neighbours snickered for three years as the brickmaker in baggy dungarees sprinkled grain for birds that did not land. Finally, in 1908, eleven geese sought sanctuary. There were thirty-two the following year. In 1910, there were 400. Gradually, the number grew to more than 50,000.

Aside from providing a safe haven, Miner also hoped to unravel the mystery of migration routes. In 1909, he banded his first duck, inscribing his address into the aluminum. Five months later he learned of the fate of the mallard, Katie, when he was notified of her death by a hunter hundreds of miles south of the sanctuary.

Miner's banding program expanded to include tens of thousands of wild ducks and Canada geese. His findings documented migration routes that spread from summer nesting grounds north of Hudson's Bay to balmy winters spent in Florida. The data contributed to the basis of the 1917 Migratory Bird Treaty between Canada and the United States, by proving that the conservation laws of the two nations had to be interrelated.

Inspired by a Salvation Army calendar, Miner began marking his bands with biblical verse as an inducement to hunters to return the bands and increase the accuracy of his migration route charts. Thousands responded to his missionary geese.

Over the next thirty years, Miner became a popular lecturer, which financed his huge feed bills and expanding conservation program. Professors compared his philosophy to that of Aristotle. He began warning of the dangers of pollution in the Great Lakes in 1927 and became the first Canadian to receive the Outdoor Life Gold Medal two years later. In celebration of the Silver Anniversary of King George V's reign, Prime Minister Mackenzie King chose Miner as Canada's representative speaker in a radio broadcast heard worldwide.

Three years after his death in 1944, the government designated the week of his birth (April 10th) as "National Wildlife Week."

His work continues through the Jack Miner Foundation, which has expanded its sanctuary from thirty-five acres to close to 400, accepting more than 125,000 visitors per year.

"There is no man so clean but what he will be a better thinking man if he gets well-acquainted with the pure, self-sacrificing ways of the Canada goose," Miner once wrote.

Golf course owners and farmers plagued by over-wintering giant Canada geese may disagree. With food readily available, thousands of geese no longer migrate.

But hope is never far off — in 1993, artist/environmentalist Bill Lishman launched a program to condition geese to migrate. Piloting an innovative ultra-light flying contraption, this modern-day Father Goose "led" an orphaned flock of eighteen geese 640 kilometres from Blackstock, Ontario to a wintering site in Virginia. Of their own accord, twelve survivors of hunters and a harsh winter returned to their birthplace near the shores of Lake Scugog. The experiment will be used as a prototype to instruct domestically-raised, endangered species such as the whooping crane in the "wild" art of migration. Jack Miner would be the first to "khonk" in approval.

THE RAIDERS OF
DRAGON BONE HILL

Zhoukoudian, China, 1927 — Who was "Peking Man?" The answer is over 300,000 years old. From fossils and artifacts unearthed by a Canadian in Chinese caves, scientists have determined that Peking Man was a critical link in the evolution of the human species. He was *homo erectus*, the first of our kind to walk upright and the first to use fire.

The discoverer of Peking Man was a Canadian named Davidson Black. He was born in Toronto in 1884 and studied medicine and arts at the University of Toronto, taking special interest in anatomy and the study of the brain. After teaching neurology in Cleveland and serving in the Canadian Army Medical Corps, he was invited to move to China as a professor of anatomy at the Peking Medical Union College.

Once in China, Black focused his attention on the anatomical study of prehistoric man, in the belief that Asia was of strategic importance in understanding the relationship between climate, evolution and the origins of the species.

There were reports of "apelike, manlike" fossil teeth being discovered in Chinese apothecary shops, where they were prized as "dragon bones" and used in curative remedies. The Chinese excavated tonnes of such bones, but without scientific purpose tracing the origins of a few molars was virtually impossible.

In 1926, at a gala scientific meeting, the discovery of two such peculiar molars by Swedish scientists at a site forty kilometres southwest of Peking (now Beijing) was revealed to great excitement. The Crown Prince of Sweden himself proposed that an expedition be mounted to explore the site known as Dragon Bone Hill near the village of Zhoukoudian. Davidson Black was nominated as the leader of the team, and the Rockefeller Foundation provided his funding.

In 1927, a army of workers excavated an entire hillside. After months of effort, one tooth was extracted.

Excavation continued and several caves were discovered. A skull was found in one of them and it was carefully removed to Black's laboratory, where he painstakingly copied it in casts. In honour of the country of their origin, Black named the specimen "Peking Man."

Numerous other fossil and tool discoveries followed, including evidence that Peking Man had developed quartz implements for skinning animals. Deep layers of ash showed early man's first use of fire.

Davidson Black, who scouted for fossils in the shale banks of Toronto's Don River as a child, earned international renown for his efforts. When he died in 1934, he was found slumped over a skull he had been working on at China's Cenozoic Research Laboratory, which he had helped found.

By the outbreak of the Second World War, over 175 specimens representing forty prehistoric individuals had been discovered at Zhoukoudian. It was the largest collection of early human fossils in the history of science.

As the war progressed, it was decided to transfer the fossils to the protection of the U.S. Marine Guard. When evacuation was ordered, the boxed fossils were prepared for embarkation on the liner *President Harrison*, but it was captured by the Japanese before leaving port.

The original fossils have never been seen again. Fortunately, the casts made by Black and his team survived and replicas of Peking Man are featured in museums throughout the world.

UNDISCOVERED COUNTRY

Montreal, 1934 — Roughly the size and shape of a cauliflower, the human brain appears to have no moving parts, although it is composed of billions of nerve cells containing a molecular structure through which electricity moves. Dr. Wilder Penfield, a passionate neurosurgeon and scientist, was a pathfinder into the mysteries of that uncharted country.

Wilder Graves Penfield was born in Spokane, Washington. His father and his father before him had been doctors. In considering his own career path, young Penfield noted that his objective in life was "to support myself and family and somehow make the world a better place in which to live." He was inexorably drawn to medicine.

At Oxford University, Penfield met the eminent Canadian physician and teacher Sir William Osler and neurophysiologist Charles Sherrington. In Osler he secured a mentor who was both a gentle healer and fearless pioneer — "a sort of John the Baptist in a wilderness of medical superstition." Sherrington introduced him to the experimental investigation of the central nervous system in which Penfield found "the undiscovered country in which the mystery of the mind might someday be explained."

In 1918, Penfield graduated from Johns Hopkins University and determined to make neurology his specialty. His work at the Presbyterian Hospital in New York fostered an interest in the causes and treatment of epilepsy — a disorder of the brain which triggers a variety of behaviours from hallucinations to seizures.

In 1928, Penfield and his neurosurgical partner, Dr. William Cone, came to work at Montreal's Royal Victoria Hospital, where they were to establish an institute devoted to neurology. A team approach, coordinated by Penfield, succeeded in binding French and English-speaking doctors and nurses in research and treatment procedures. According to Penfield: "The study of the brain is a field that a man could no more explore alone than he could paddle his way to the North Pole in a canvas canoe."

Penfield experienced one of his greatest and most tragic challenges in Montreal. His sister, Ruth, had suffered epileptic seizures throughout her life, but these were often attributed to "nerves" — the catch-all phrase for anything medical science could not fathom. Ruth's condition was growing critical and Penfield determined to operate.

He discovered a massive brain tumour, which proved too large to remove in its entirety. Nevertheless, the young woman lived for three more years. "The resentment I felt because of my inability to save my sister spurred me on to make my first bid for an endowed neurological institute," noted Penfield.

In 1934, Wilder Penfield became a Canadian citizen. In the same year, the Montreal Neurological Institute opened with the words of its founder engraved on a stone slab to mark the occasion. "Dedicated to the relief of sickness and pain and to the study of neurology," wrote Penfield, who was to be the Institute's director until 1960.

In Montreal, Penfield perfected a technique for

removing scar tissue that caused forms of epilepsy in the temporal lobes. Applying only a local anesthetic, he would probe the exposed brain, relying on the response of the patient to guide him. Brain tissue itself has no sensations, but it recognizes sensations sent to it from other parts of the body and the stimulus of a mild electrical current to the specific points in the surface of the brain triggers certain responses. By stimulating the temporal lobe, Penfield discovered the source of memory, the mind's reservoir of sensation and emotion, and the storehouse of dreams.

In the space of thirty years, Penfield operated on more than 750 patients suffering from epilepsy. Despite improvements in technology and refinements in techniques, the operating procedure used today remains remarkably similar to that performed by Penfield in the 1930s.

"It is the patients who can teach one the most," Penfield wrote in his autobiography *No Man Alone*. "They open their hearts and minds. And the doctor, if he will only listen, comes to understand the inborn nature of man."

PART 7

TRANSPORTATION AND COMMUNICATION

THE TELEGRAPH AT HEART'S CONTENT

Heart's Content, Newfoundland, 1866 — When the telegraph came to Canada in 1846, people called it "talk by lightning," and a revolution in communication began. Current events were suddenly "current" outside of their immediate locality. Life-saving messages were sent and chess games transpired between counties. Prince Edward Island made telegraphic communication to the mainland a condition of its entry into Confederation, and telegraph lines took their place along with railway tracks, merging transportation and communication across the nation.

Like the construction of the railways, laying telegraph lines across the nation's jumble of geography was a feat of epic proportion. And the laying of a cable across the Atlantic Ocean from England to Newfoundland ranks as one of the outstanding achievements of the nineteenth century. It began as the dream of a self-educated, English civil engineer named Frederick Newton Gisborne, but the thunder and the glory of its success were usurped by an American tycoon.

Gisborne kicked around the world touring places such as Australia, Tahiti, Guatemala and Mexico before settling on a farm at St. Eustache, Lower Canada in 1845. Two years later, the twenty-five-year-old abandoned the plough in favour of a more exciting career in telegraphy. Shortly afterward, the understanding of electrical principles applied to communications that he had studied in books, saw him supervising the construction of telegraph lines. By 1849, he had become chief operator and superintendent of the Nova Scotia Telegraph Company, and in 1852 he laid the first submarine cable in British North America, connecting Prince Edward Island and New Brunswick.

Never one to rest on his laurels, he formed the New York, Newfoundland and London Telegraph Company and surveyed 640 kilometres of the rugged island with a stipend blessing from the Newfoundland government. Ultimately, he found himself $50,000 in debt in the midst of laying an overland line. His property was confiscated and he was arrested.

But the dreamer would not quit. Years before he had discussed the prospect of trans-Atlantic telegraphy with Nova Scotia Premier Joseph Howe. Flat broke, Gisborne headed for New York to find investors. Late one January evening in 1854, he met Cyrus Field.

Field had made a fortune in the U.S. paper industry and was a bored millionaire at thirty-three. Gisborne's venture was a new challenge. Four months after their first meeting, Field had drafted a company and subscribed 1.5 million dollars for the project. Gisborne's affairs were settled, and he was put on the payroll as Chief Engineer, but he lost control of the dream.

Where Gisborne had employed 350 workers on the overland Newfoundland line, Field hired 600 to confront the irregular landscape. By the end of 1856, more than a million dollars had been spent, and Field kept raising more. Despite chronic seasickness, he made more than forty trips to England seeking support and advice. Two attempts to lay a cable across the ocean failed, although communications stayed clear for four weeks in August 1858 before a spasm silenced the flawed line.

The Civil War postponed further development, but in July 1865 Field was back at it. A stronger, more flexible cable weighing almost twice as much as the original was constructed and Field chartered the largest ship in the world to lay it. When the *Great Eastern* left Ireland, she carried a crew of 500, more than 8,000 tonnes of coal, a milk cow and assorted livestock including 120 sheep. They were less than a day away from the safe harbour of Heart's Content, Newfoundland when the cable snapped. Field raised another three million dollars and built more cable.

On July 27, 1866, the *Great Eastern* finally delivered her payload. Cheering spectators lofted Field into the village for celebrations that spread throughout the island. A few weeks later, the previous cable was salvaged and connected. Although it cost the equivalent of $100 to send a twenty-word message, more than 2,700 were sent in the first two months.

Cyrus Field began taking credit as the originator of the Atlantic cable scheme soon after a disheartened Frederick Gisborne resigned in 1857. Typically, debate ensued over who was the "father of the mighty thought," but Gisborne avoided the pettiness. He studied geology in New Zealand. He invented a shipboard flag-and-ball semaphore. In the Middle East, he was involved in laying cable across the Red Sea and, by the 1870s, he was back in Nova Scotia as a railroader. In 1879, he was appointed as superintendent of the Dominion Telegraph and Signal Service, and, before he died in 1892, he told a friend that he had a vision of a time "when messages will be sent across the Atlantic *through the air*." Dreamers can see such things.

"GET A HORSE!"

Rustico, Prince Edward Island, 1866 — What was supposed to be a quiet Sunday celebration became an historic event, when Father George Belacourt surprised his Island parishioners by arriving in a steam-propelled vehicle, which is believed to have been the first of its kind in British North America.

The vehicle Father Belacourt imported from New Jersey was a great crowd pleaser. The mobile priest made several demonstration runs and the *Charlottetown Examiner* reported: "With wonder and delight it was observed steaming away... at a fast speed."

The witnessing of the dawn of a new era of transportation ended when the priest lost control of the newfangled contraption and veered into a field.

The following year, Henry Seth Taylor of Stanstead, Quebec built Canada's first steam carriage and the local newspaper was quick to pronounce it "the neatest thing of its kind yet invented."

The first electric automobile in Canada appeared on the streets of Toronto in December 1893. A local company built the battery-powered vehicle for lawyer Frederick Fetherstonhaugh, who proudly demonstrated its ability to travel to speeds of up to twenty-four kilometres per hour.

Motoring began to acquire an aura of glamour characterized by speed. A three-wheel car from France driven by a Quebec dentist reached the "dizzying" speed of twenty-nine kilometres per hour in an 1897 demonstration along Chemin Sainte-Foy. In the same year, George Foote Foss, a bicycle repairman from Sherbrooke, constructed Canada's first gasoline driven car for his personal use. He drove it summer and winter for five years, and got more than eighty kilometres to the gallon.

Hamilton's Colonel John Moodie Jr. acquired the first "mass market" gasoline-engine car in April 1898. It looked for all the world like a horse-drawn buggy, with the engine in the rear. Moodie's "Winton" was such a novelty that he installed spikes around the ends to deter unwanted passengers. He once raced a steamboat from Hamilton to Toronto, winning in just less than three hours.

Despite the outrageous price tag of $1,000, Colonel Moodie contended that his car was cheaper to own than a pair of good horses. In fact, his "horseless carriage" stayed in use for fifteen years.

At the turn of the century, dozens of small machine shops had blossomed into car-makers, but many people still thought cars were a noisy and unreliable fad. Inexperienced drivers wrecked havoc on narrow roadways and the unfamiliar sound of backfires caused horses to bolt, and bicyclists to topple.

"Infernally combusting engines" became the constant butt of jokes and the roadside taunt of the day was "get a horse." In schools, a favourite topic of debate was "Resolved: That the Motor-Car is Useless, Dangerous and Ought to be Abolished."

Prince Edward Island, in particular, did not take kindly to automobiles. In 1908, the Legislature voted to ban all autos in response to citizens' concerns about wear and tear to the roadways and the terrorization of livestock and children. "We're going to keep them cars out if we have to take a pitchfork to them," wrote one Island farmer.

Canada's love affair with the horseless carriage could not be suppressed. Ford started manufacturing cars in Canada in 1903 and Oshawa carriage maker Sam McLaughlin turned out the nation's first all-Canadian Buick in 1908. By 1911, the T. Eaton Company was selling mail-order automobiles.

The automobile became an industry, as well as a national passion. From 1920 to 1930, the number of cars, trucks, buses and motorcycles increased three-fold to 1,235,000, making Canada the second most-motorized country on the globe after the United States. Within a decade, the number of concrete or blacktopped roads rose from 1,000 to 9,200. Still, a new word managed to find its way into the lexicon. The original "traffic jam" described autos stuck up to their hubcaps in mud on rural roads.

BLOOD ON THE TRACKS

Yale, British Columbia, 1880 — Whoever thinks of Canada's history as explosive? But it was — literally and figuratively. For instance, nitro-glycerine played a very significant part in the unification of Canada.

This awesomely unstable liquid was used to blast through mountains of granite during the construction of the national railway system, and hundreds of the 30,000 workers who toiled on the railway died setting the explosive charges that carved the groundwork for tracks from sea to shining sea.

There are segments of the Canadian landscape where nature seemed to have gone to extremes to thwart the railway builders. Muskeg, bogs and sinkholes presented their own unique problems, but when it came to the Rockies the builders confronted wrinkled canyons, criss-crossed by deadfalls and sheer walls rising to lofty heights above rushing rivers.

An American named Andrew Onderdonk purchased the contracts to build the railway line west of the Fraser

Valley. In 1880 he established his headquarters at Yale, British Columbia on the Fraser River. There were four tunnels to be drilled within a three kilometer radius and it took eighteen months to blast them out of the rock of the canyon. Twenty-three more tunnels were drilled on the Onderdonk line.

Onderdonk built an explosives factory at Yale. When the factory blew up, shattering every window in the town, Onderdonk simply shrugged his shoulders and built another factory. By 1882, the Yale factory was turning out nearly two tonnes of nitro-glycerine a day.

Hell's Gate on the Fraser was aptly named according to the "navvies" who blasted holes into the rock face above a sheer drop into the foaming waters below. Men had to be lowered on ladders secured by ropes which were attached to trees on the summit until they reached the level where the tracks were to be placed. The canyon walls were slick, so they worked in bare feet to try for better footing, but the hard rock surface often frayed critically on the rope. Falling rocks or a premature blast could mean certain death.

Blasting holes were drilled into the granite, which was striped with quartz — the hardest of all rocks. Once the charge was set, the worker was hauled to the surface or he took refuge in a "secure" hiding place. Then the fuse was lit.

None of this work took place under ideal circumstances and some of the workers did not make it when the charges failed to do what they were supposed to do. Some men died when explosions were improperly timed, and rocks had a dangerous habit of catapulting off the canyon walls and into the "hiding" places. Rock slides and avalanches were triggered by the continual blasting.

Most of the railway workers had no previous experience with explosives or safety provisions.

One tried to light his pipe after handling blasting powder. Others were killed when they vigorously dumped dynamite down a chute into a waiting boat. One Chinese worker near Yale hid behind a tree sixty metres from a tunnel that was to be blasted, only to have a flying splinter shear off his nose.

Fortunes were made and boundless opportunities were opened by the building of the railway. But the human price in the lives of the labourers — French and English, Scots and Irish, Italians and Slavs, Swedes and Americans, Canadians and Chinese — was exacted in an immeasurable toll that was written in blood on the tracks.

DOT, DOT, DOT...!

Signal Hill, Newfoundland, 1901 — There he was, thirteen days before Christmas, a grown man flying a kite on Signal Hill in the middle of a storm. And, if one man wasn't fool enough, he had a couple of buddies helping him out. But the fool on the hill was no fool at all. He was Guglielmo Marconi and the kite he was hoisting on a 180-metre wire would serve as an aerial for the first wireless signal to be sent across the Atlantic Ocean.

At the time of Marconi's birth in Italy in 1874, Alexander Graham Bell was trying to perfect the invention of the telephone. By the age of thirteen, Guglielmo (or William) had begun to experiment with scientific principles. One of his first creations was a whisky still, which may not be surprising since his maternal grandfather was Irish whisky czar Andrew Jameson. His fascination quickly transferred to electricity. After completing a biography of Benjamin Franklin, he rigged some dinner plates on wires at the edge of a stream. Using a homemade battery, he passed a high-tension, electric current through the wires, causing the plates to "jump" and smash into smithereens.

Marconi's studies included practical experiments at the University of Bologna and summer holidays learning Morse code. At twenty-one, he succeeded in transmitting a wireless Morse code message over three kilometres across the family estate. Initially, Marconi foresaw that his new system of communication could be of great use linking ships at sea with shore bases. When the Italian government indicated that they were not interested, Marconi took his invention to England.

In 1896, he demonstrated his wireless transmission to British experts from the Army, Navy and Post Office. "The calm of my life ended then," he told a friend. Overnight, he became a famous figure. Offers poured in for his patented invention, but he would not sell. Marconi continued his experiments in Britain, extending the range to almost twenty kilometres.

In 1898, the British first employed wireless telegraphy between lightships and shore installations. Realizing that his invention needed popular support, Marconi arranged with a Dublin newspaper to provide the world's first radio sports report, covering a yachting race that summer. The publicity was tremendous. Queen Victoria herself read the accounts and requested the installation of a personal wireless device so that she could communicate with the Prince of Wales' yacht from the Royal residence on the Isle of Wight.

As the story goes, Marconi was fixing equipment one day and doffed his hat as the Queen walked by, a liberty which the monarch found offensive. A gardener instructed Marconi to leave by the back way, which he found offensive. Confronted with this state of affairs, Victoria is said to have replied haughtily: "Get another electrician." She later reconsidered, giving Marconi both an audience and her wishes for success.

After numerous experiments, Marconi was convinced

that he could achieve a wireless link between Britain and North America. With typical, boyish enthusiasm he called it "the big thing." Although many in the scientific community were sceptical, he was able to persuade the investors of Marconi's Wireless Telegraph Company Ltd. to finance his new venture.

A land station was established at Pohdhu in Cornwall in 1900 and Marconi was able to transmit over 380 kilometres. Subsequently, he tried to establish a receiving station in Cape Cod, but it was wiped out by a storm. Undaunted, Marconi ordered another station to be set up at St. John's in Newfoundland and his assistants scouted the Signal Hill location.

At first, they tried using a huge balloon filled with hydrogen gas to raise the 180-metre wire aerial, but strong winds snapped its mooring rope. Marconi suggested trying kites. The first rose to 135 metres before it shared the balloon's fate. Finally on December 12, 1901, the kite soared to its full height. The crew retired to a small building equipped with a table, one chair and Marconi's equipment. Pohdhu station was transmitting the Morse code letter "S" (dot, dot, dot) regularly for a fixed period.

With a gale in full progress, Marconi adjusted his earphone and started listening. Shortly after noon, "the big thing" became a reality as Marconi heard the three-dot transmission from Pohdhu and his assistants gathered to listen to the $200,000 signal that crossed the ocean.

Cable companies that owned communication rights in Newfoundland forced Marconi to leave the island soon after his historic triumph. However, Prime Minister Sir Wilfrid Laurier stepped in to save the day. The Canadian government provided Marconi with $80,000 to continue his experiments at Glace Bay, Nova Scotia. One year later Governor General Minto sent the first wireless transmission from Canada to Britain.

A new age of communication had begun.

GETTING THROUGH THE DRIFT

Montreal, 1925 — The Inuit language contains twenty-three separate words for "snow." The great frozen flakes have always been both a wonderment and a scourge of the vast Canadian landscape. As Quebec songwriter Gilles Vigneault noted in the first line of his popular 1965 song "Mon Pays": "My country is not a country: it's winter!"

Snow posed many historic dilemmas in the exploration and settlement of Canada. While the native people of North America adapted to the dictates of nature and the rhythms of climatic change, European settlers were determined to go against the drift.

The problem presented itself most dramatically in 1885, when the Canadian Pacific Railway was completed. Snowslides, avalanche debris and drifts two-storys high closed the line through the Rocky Mountains for months at a time. Conventional wedge-ploughs were no match for such conditions.

A Toronto dentist, J. W. Elliot, took out a patent on the "Compound Revolving Snow Shovel" in 1869. Elliot's theory involved using rotary blades to slice through packed snow, but he was unable to find investors.

Fourteen years later, a fellow inventor named Orange Jull supervised the first working model of a rotary plough that was tested at the CPR yards in Toronto. Soon afterward, the Elliot-Jull snowplough became standard equipment on trains throughout North America. But it took the ingenuity of a young Quebec farmer who just wanted to get his milk to market before it soured to invent the snowblower.

Arthur Sicard was an orphan who was trying to earn his keep on a farm near St. Leonard de Port Maurice when he discovered the frustration of drifting snow. After milking the cows at dawn, he would load the milk cans into a horse-drawn sleigh to begin the eight kilometer trek to market in Montreal. When faced with an impassable road, Sicard would be forced to return through the bitter cold. If poor weather continued, the milk would go bad, adding financial loss to frustration.

Sicard was determined to find a solution. When he was eighteen, working in the harvest fields, he observed an inspirational machine — a thresher. It separated the grain from the straw by shaking, screening and blowing the chaff away. Sicard reasoned that the same sort of blowing principle could work on snow.

Despite the derision of neighbours, he devoted himself to experimenting and tinkering with machinery throughout that winter. In addition to the rotating blades of the threshing machine, Sicard added a fan to push the snow back into the blades, forcing it out through a discharge chute.

The following year, in 1895, Sicard was ready to demonstrate his device. While a curious crowd stood witness, Sicard blew away small snow drifts, but bogged down in large ones. The crowd laughed and went home, but Sicard persisted.

Using his own savings, he quietly worked on perfecting the machine. His fellow farmers considered him a crackpot, so he went to work in Montreal as a labourer in the construction industry, and later as a road contractor.

Finally, in 1925, Sicard displayed his snow-blowing device. The lumbering vehicle featured a conventional truck cab, with an auxiliary motor in the body. Two rotating blades replaced the bumpers and they spewed snow behind through a long ejection shoot, leaving a cleared path for traffic. No one was laughing now.

Various Quebec municipalities purchased Sicard's snowblowers. The Department of Transport in Ottawa also saw their virtues, and eventually his snowblowers were clearing everything from roads to airport runways throughout the world.

Canadian ingenuity had conquered the snow drift.

THE HAPPY NEW YEAR MISSION

Fort Vermilion, Alberta, 1929 — There are many legendary bush pilots in the annals of Canadian aviation. At the drop of a hat, these winged *coureurs de bois* would fly, navigating over the wilderness "by the seat of their pants" and "improvising" when it came to repairs. Among them Wilfred Reid "Wop" May is a classic example. The stuff of true romance, he flew what everyone considered to be a doomed mission of mercy one frozen New Year's Eve to the northern reaches of wild Alberta with antitoxin for a village threatened by an epidemic of diphtheria.

From the beginning, flying was an adventure for May. On his first World War One combat mission, he shot down an enemy aircraft. Then May's guns jammed and he found himself being chased by the German ace, Baron Manfred von Richthofen. Captain Roy Brown, one of May's Alberta school chums, shot down Richtofen and saved his friend from becoming the eighty-first victim of the Red Baron.

After the war, May settled in Edmonton and started a commercial aviation business, along with daring "barnstorming" exhibitions. He was one of the founding members of the Edmonton and Northern Alberta Aero Club.

All of May's skill and ingenuity were called on when he was asked to fly a mercy mission on the bitterly cold New Year's Day of 1929. On December 15th, a Hudson Bay Company employee in Little Red River, north of Fort Vermilion, died of diphtheria. Other cases were breaking out and vaccine was desperately needed to prevent an epidemic in the community of about 300 people.

The nearest radio station was at Peace River, and Louis Bourassa, the postal courier, set out on a 450 kilometre dog sled trip to send the urgent request. Fourteen days later, Dr. M. H. Bow, Deputy Minister of the Department of Health, received the telegraphed message in Edmonton. He calculated that it would take at least two weeks by train and dog sled to deliver the necessary supplies. A fly-in mission seemed the only answer, and Dr. Bow posed the question to "Wop" May, who agreed without hesitation.

Emergency workers gathered the life-saving serum while May and his co-pilot Vic Horner prepared to make the 990 kilometre trip. The only airplane available to them was Horner's small Avro biplane which boasted a seventy-five horsepower engine, an open cockpit, and no skiis for winter landing. To protect the vaccine from freezing, it was placed in an improvised thermal unit consisting of heated containers balanced on a portable charcoal stove and covered with blankets.

Blizzard conditions forced them to land on a frozen lake at McLennan Junction, almost halfway to Fort Vermilion. May realized that he would have to remove the plane's oil to prevent it from congealing, but he did not have a container. Undaunted, he siphoned the oil onto the crusty snow where it froze immediately. May carried the "oilsicle" to the village, where it thawed overnight.

When the pair arrived in Fort Vermilion the following

day, their precious cargo was protected, but May and Horner were so frost-bitten and chilled that they had to be physically removed from the cockpit. The serum was dispersed by dog sled to the anxious community and the epidemic was checked.

The homeward trip brought its own complications. The whole plane was coated with ice, instruments froze and the engine cut out several times due to low-grade gasoline. All the while, the media hailed their courageous "gamble with death."

A crowd of 5,000 was on hand to greet the heroes when they returned to Edmonton and May was awarded the prestigious McKee Trophy for his efforts. Six years later he was created an Officer of the Order of the British Empire, and mail-carrier Louis Bourassa was honoured as a Member of the same Order. May went on to pioneer aerial search-and-rescue techniques and he helped set up the British Commonwealth Air Training Plan during World War Two.

The bush pilots of Canada's north helped the nation enter into a new era of transportation and communication. Wilfred Reid May, who was nicknamed "Wop" by a baby cousin who could not pronounce "Wilfred," was one of the best.

HAVE SKI-DOO WILL TRAVEL

Valcourt, Quebec, 1935 — Joseph-Armand Bombardier gave new meaning to the concept of "dashing through the snow." He unlocked the world of winter when he created the snowmobile.

Bombardier grew up in the community of Valcourt in Quebec's Eastern Townships. Throughout his childhood he enjoyed nothing better than constructing machinery.

On New Year's Eve 1922, Bombardier demonstrated his first snowmobile. His father had given him an old automobile, and Bombardier promptly removed the engine, which he mounted on four runners. A large, hand-made propeller replaced the radiator fan. Joseph-Armand perched on the back, while his brother Léopold was in front, steering with his feet. To the astonishment of his neighbours, Bombardier "drove" his primitive snowmobile through the centre of Valcourt. It was a dangerous contraption, but the young mechanical genius became convinced that it was possible for a man and a machine to conquer transportation over snow.

Bombardier continued to tinker with mechanical inventions. He learned English so that he could decipher technical journals. At nineteen, his father built him his own garage, which grew into a successful business. His passion remained the production of snow machine prototypes, but tragedy was to provide his ultimate impetus.

In 1934, his son, Yvon, died following an attack of appendicitis during a bitter winter storm. Roads were blocked with snow and Bombardier's various snow machines were lying in pieces in the garage. There was no way to transport the child to the hospital. With the loss of his son, Bombardier focused in earnest on the invention he had dreamed of since childhood.

The following year he designed and built a rubber-cushioned drive-wheel and track. With a model that satisfied him, he began a series of demonstrations that exhibited his impressive marketing skills as well as his remarkable invention. Travelling from town to town throughout Quebec, he invited local newspaper editors for a ride and became front-page news wherever he went. Two years later, he was granted his first patent for a snowmobile called B7 — B for Bombardier and 7 for the number of passengers it could carry. Full-scale manufacturing began in 1942.

The snowmobile was an immediate success — priests, country doctors and ambulance drivers quickly bought the new machines. Soon, "Bombardiers" were transporting everything from mail to medical rescue crews. During the Second World War, the vehicle was modified for military purposes and a twelve-passenger model gained international and commercial acceptance.

In 1959, Bombardier introduced a sport model. He considered calling the two-passenger version the "ski-dog," before settling on the now famous "Ski-Doo." By the late 1960s, ski-dooing had captured the popular imagination and revolutionized transportation in northern communities. Five years after Bombardier's death in 1964, the

Royal Canadian Mounted Police replaced their last Yukon sled dog teams with snowmobiles.

Competing brands of snowmobiles threatened to overwhelm the family firm in the early 1970s, however, Bombardier's heirs shared the innovative spirit of their founder. In 1974, Bombardier Inc. diversified and entered the public transit business, manufacturing 423 subway cars for the city of Montreal. Eight years later, Bombardier signed a multi-million dollar contract to supply subway cars to New York City. Subsequently, the corporation has expanded into aeronautics and high-speed trains, but recreational activities remain at the forefront of operations. In 1988, the company introduced the "Sea-Doo," which demonstrates the same agility on the water as its snow conquering counterpart.

Bombardier's inventions have been used in building dikes in Holland, herding reindeer in Lapland, laying pipelines in Scotland and hauling logs in the Peruvian jungle. But to millions of red-cheeked Canadians, Joseph-Armand Bombardier is remembered quite simply as the man who made winter fun.

As It Happened

Moose River, Nova Scotia, 1936 — In what has been lauded as the outstanding radio news story of the first half of the twentieth century, J. Frank Willis of the fledgling Canadian Radio Broadcasting Commission (CRBC), reported every half hour from April 20, 1936 for sixty-nine hours to fifty-eight Canadian stations and 650 American stations, while Nova Scotia draegermen struggled to save lives at a remote collapsed mine at Moose River. His broadcast held a staggering fifty million listeners across North America spellbound for almost three days.

On Easter Sunday in 1936, two Toronto men, Dr. David Roberston, chief surgeon at the Hospital for Sick Children and lawyer Herman Magill, went to inspect a sixty-year-old gold mine they had bought in Moose River, ninety kilometres northeast of Halifax.

With their timekeeper, Alfred Scadding, the men descended, unaware that the shaft was barely supported by rotting timbers. After about an hour, the noise of shifting rock alarmed them. At the forty-two-metre level, the mine buckled and the men were trapped in a dark, wet cave.

A rescue mission was immediately launched, but by April 15th newspaper headlines mourned "Hope Almost Gone." While miners attempted to tunnel toward the men, diamond driller Billy Bell succeeded in opening a shaft approximately four centimetres in diameter on April 18th. Just before midnight, a small steam whistle was used to attempt to signal the men, and at 12:30 a.m., Billy Bell heard a tapping response on the pipe and hope was renewed.

Food, candles and medicine were lowered to the men, and hot soup was passed through a rubber tube. Using the shell of a penlight flashlight as a casing, foreman Bill Boak, and engineer W. E. Jefferson, of the Maritime Telegraph and Telephone Company, improvised a miniature microphone. It too was sent down the drill hole providing telephone communication with the ever-weakening men, who spoke to their wives.

Newspaper reporters had already swarmed the site, when Willis, the only CRBC employee east of Montreal, arrived on April 20th. Although Michael Dwyer, Minister of Mines for Nova Scotia, had commandeered the only local telephone line for the rescue, he granted Willis permission to use it for several minutes every half hour for a broadcast.

Between the Canadian network and the U.S. station coverage, almost anyone on the North American continent who could get to a radio could hear what was going on as it happened. Willis reported from the mouth of the hole, interviewing draegermen as they crawled out for any word about the progress.

On the first day of Willis' marathon broadcast, Herman Magill died from exposure. Prayerful listeners were glued to their radios. Teachers set up radios in their classrooms. Doctors reported increases in patients with "nervous prostration," suffering from too much excitement and too many late nights. In his rich baritone, Willis reported "the torture of doubt, the Calvary of mental anguish, the nerve-destroying sound of dripping water, the rattle and splash of falling rocks."

Not everyone was enthralled with Willis' reporting. On April 21st, Nova Scotia Premier Angus Macdonald fired off a blistering telegraph of complaint to CRBC headquarters in Ottawa. In it he complained about the "inaccurate, exaggerated and over-dramatized nature of some radio comments." But Willis persisted until he was able to announce the most-awaited of messages: "The long-looked-for victory is now in our hands, and those men are coming out alive!"

In the early hours of April 22nd, the two grateful survivors were brought to the surface, where the miners sang "Praise God from Whom All Blessings Come."

"We are cutting our wires now and heading back," advised a weary Willis. The drama was over, but through it the Canadian Radio Broadcasting Commission had come of age. Six months later, the Canadian Broadcasting Corporation came into being.

THE CROSS-DISCIPLINE
DRESSER

Toronto, 1965 — Few, if any, Canadian thinkers have ever been mentioned in the same breath as Freud and Einstein. "Suppose he is what he sounds like — the most important thinker since Newton, Darwin, Freud, Einstein, and Pavlov — suppose he is the Oracle of Modern Times?" Tom Wolfe postulated in an article about Marshall McLuhan for *New York* magazine entitled "What If He's Right?" But the big question with McLuhan has always been "right about what?"

In spite of the fact that most people did not, and do not, understand one iota of what he wrote or said, Marshall McLuhan is one of the few men in the twentieth century who became truly famous for his ideas alone. Take Sigmund Freud, for example, whom everyone considers another "oracle of the modern times."

Although both Freud and McLuhan are virtually household names, most people are willing to believe Freud's idea that there is a dark side to the human psyche for which the individual is not consciously responsible. But few, if any, understand what McLuhan meant when he wrote that "the medium is the message" in *Understanding Media*, published in 1964. Besides, Freud was from Vienna, the zenith of European culture and learning.

Herbert Marshall McLuhan was born in Edmonton, Alberta on July 11, 1911. By the time he died in Toronto on December 31, 1980, he was the most famous man of letters Canada has ever produced.

He had the ear of captains of industry around the world. His opinions were regularly sought out by heads of state. Revered as a teacher and often reviled by his peers, McLuhan also loved jokes and one-liners. One of his favourites was about the first telephone pole — Alexander Graham Kowalski.

Because he was a true prankster, McLuhan pretended to put more stock in his participation in the popular culture than he did in the machinations of academia. He was inordinately proud of his walk-on part in Woody Allen's 1977 film *Annie Hall*. He took great delight in the fact that he was regularly mentioned on *Laugh-In*, an enormously popular 1960s television comedy series. In the middle of every show, one of the stand-up comedians would suddenly crop up on the screen and pose the philosophical question: "Marshall McLuhan, what'er ya doin'?"

He wrote articles for magazines such as *TV Guide*, *Family Circle*, *Glamour*, *Vogue*, *The Saturday Evening Post*, and *Playboy*, publications in which no self-respecting academic would be caught, even posthumously, although they all secretly wished for such popular recognition of their work. The Beatles thought McLuhan was cool, but he, undoubtedly, thought they were "hot."

To McLuhan, his role in the popular culture as "Guru of the Global Village" was completely consistent with his other roles as academic, thinker and teacher. The thematic underpinnings of McLuhan's theories are really quite simple: to McLuhan, everything was a medium, not just the obvious such as the telephone or the newspaper. A railroad was a medium. Money was a medium. Furs were a medium. Victims of fashion were aphorisms of insight. Nothing escaped: the wheel, the spear, the stirrup. All were media.

He contended that change and the individual's relationship to the world was not driven by war, religion or politics, but by the inexorable and invisible force of new media.

When he first reportedly said "the medium is the message" at a reception following a symposium on music and the mass media at the University of British Columbia in 1959, he simply meant that the key to understanding the world in which we live is contained in the technique and technology of new media. For instance, to know the message of the miraculous invention of television, the student must first comprehend the world before television. The message of the medium of television is the effect it has on the individual and society and its effects cannot be understood unless one understands what life was like B.T.V. (Before Television). For McLuhan, the fastest way to gain an understanding of different cultures or different times was through the period's poets, writers and artists.

By training McLuhan was an English teacher and he looked every inch the part. He was tall, with a long straight face and appropriately pallid complexion. He combed his hair straight back. If he could be said to have had a disposition, he would have been described as perpetually preoccupied. Slightly dishevelled, he worked out of a small, dilapidated office on the edge of the University of Toronto. He taught English to freshman and graduate students alike. Even at the height of his fame, he graded papers himself.

McLuhan saw poets as seers, society's antenna, and claimed he derived most, if not all, of his insights from their study. He had an uncanny ability to discover in the work of difficult writers such as Gerald Manley Hopkins, Ezra Pound and James Joyce, delightful insights into the modern world and everyday life. In doing so, he made the writers' works more accessible to his students.

McLuhan was a kind of professional student himself. After graduating from the University of Manitoba in 1933, he went to England and took a second undergraduate degree in 1936. He eventually got his doctorate from Cambridge in 1943. His first teaching job was at the University of Wisconsin in 1936. An A-1 classification from a draft board in St. Louis in 1943 propelled him back to teaching positions in Canada.

His first book, *The Mechanical Bride*, was published in 1951. The book was didactic and argued that a technologically driven society destroys family life and the free expression of thought and feeling. The book did not do at all well. From then on, he abandoned point-of-view and argued that all of his statements, insights and attitudes were merely "probes."

In 1952 he teamed up with his friend and colleague, anthropologist Edmund Carpenter and that collaboration eventually produced *Explorations in Communications*. He went on to participate in many collaborations: with Quentin Fiore for two books, *The Medium is the Message* and *War and Peace in the Global Village*; *The Marshall McLuhan DEW-LINE Newsletter* with Eugene Swartz and *Through the Vanishing Point* with his friend Harley Parker. McLuhan was astonishingly widely read. An eclectic and an inordinately curious man, he could truly dress across disciplines.

In the late 1950s, he had come under the influence of a University of Toronto historian named Harold Innis who wrote books about the fur trade in Canada with titles such as *The Bias of Communication*.

In his preface to *The Gutenberg Galaxy* (1962), McLuhan gave Innis his due: "Innis explained why print causes nationalism and not tribalism; and why print causes price systems and markets such as cannot exist without print. In short, Harold Innis was the first person to hit upon the process of change as implicit in the form of media technology. The present book is a footnote of explanation to his work." McLuhan's "footnote" won the Governor General's Award for non-fiction. It was followed by *Understanding Media* (1964) and *The Medium is the Message* in 1967. These books formed a body of work that brought him international fame.

It was partly the temper of the times and partly good management — McLuhan's career as a consultant and public speaker was managed by a remarkable San Francisco public relations duo, Gerald Feigen and Howard Gossage. The more unintelligible and aphoristic McLuhan became, the more in demand and famous.

Giant corporations such as IBM, GE, Bell Telephone and others paid inordinate sums to have him lecture their senior executives about the unseen world of the electronic environment. He was fond of saying "they all know just about exactly nothing about the real business that they are in." The more he said stuff like that, the more they paid him.

In 1963 he became the director of the Centre for Culture and Technology, which was a fancy name for what was essentially a one-man band with some letterhead. It was eventually set up in a coach house on an alleyway behind the library of the St. Michael's College campus at the University of Toronto.

No matter how far he travelled or how widely he was championed, how much he was paid, or how famous he became, he always returned to his dishevelled coach house and the classroom. His true legacy takes two forms: the Centre for Culture and Technology, which has become a hub of international inquiry into the effects of mass media, and the thousands of students in whom he instilled perpetual curiosity, eclecticism and a unique understanding of poetry.

"You don't like these ideas?... I got others." Thus spoke Marshall McLuhan.